To Hear
Celestial Harmonies

To Hear Celestial Harmonies

Essays on the Witness of James DeKoven and The DeKoven Center

Sesquicentennial Edition

Edited by

Robert Boak Slocum
and Travis Talmadge Du Priest

WIPF & STOCK · Eugene, Oregon

Wipf and Stock Publishers
199 W 8th Ave, Suite 3
Eugene, OR 97401

To Hear Celestial Harmonies
Essays on the Witness of James DeKoven and The DeKoven Center,
Sesquicentennial Edition 1852 - 2002
By Slocum, Robert Boak and DuPriest, Travis T.
Copyright©2002 by Slocum, Robert Boak
ISBN 13: 978-1-4982-0235-0
Publication date 9/8/2014
Previously published by Forward Movement Publications, 2002

Dedication

This book is dedicated to
Mr. William Lewis and Mrs. Josephine McNeil Lewis,
Longtime Friends of The DeKoven Center and
Patrons of the Sesquicentennial Celebrations,
whose generous gift made possible
the completion and publication of this work.

Table Of Contents

Dedication v

Acknowledgements ix

Preface xi

1. Biography of James DeKoven
   by Lawrence N. Crumb 1

2. Romantic Religion and the
   Witness of James DeKoven
   by Robert Boak Slocum 15

3. James DeKoven, Novelist, A Review
   by Mabel Benson Du Priest 33

4. A Brief History of Racine College
   by Jason Fout 47

5. The Middle Watch
   by Katherine Greer Clark 63

6. The DeKoven Center, 1958-1986
   by Sister Dorcas Baker, C.S.M. 71

7. DeKoven: Holy Man, Holy Place
   by Travis Talmadge Du Priest 93

8. Contributors 104

Acknowledgements

The editors are grateful to all who contributed essays for this project and to Dorothy Osborne whose on-going research and writing on Racine College is an inspiration. We also want to acknowledge Phil Duncan for his technical assistance in preparing the book for publication and Julia Peyton for her research in the photographic archives of The DeKoven Center which made possible the publication of historic photographs in this book.

Robert Boak Slocum
Travis Talmadge Du Priest

Preface

"The Fragments and the Whole"

As he was nearing the end of his life, James DeKoven preached a sermon titled "Gathering the Fragments." I strongly suspect that when DeKoven prepared this particular sermon, he felt that he was looking back over the fragments of his life. From our perspective, we see clearly how his life and witness engaged and shaped the Episcopal Church with a vision of inclusiveness where a variety of perspectives and practices can be honored. We can see how his ministry is continued today through the work of The DeKoven Center, and how his life touched and continues to touch those who seek God's love and who seek to be of service to humanity. But I think his perspective must have been very different. He was nominated to be bishop in several dioceses, but he never became a bishop. In the Diocese of Wisconsin, his own former colleagues at Nashotah House led the opposition to his election. When he was finally elected in the Diocese of Illinois, the necessary consents to his election could not be obtained from the other dioceses of the Episcopal Church. And the opposition was based on challenges to his orthodoxy as a Christian believer. This must have been painful to him.

Ignatian spirituality describes the alternation of times of consolation and desolation in each life. The celebration of the Sesquicentennial of The DeKoven Center in 2002 is certainly an occasion of great encouragement and consolation. But we must remember that the witness of DeKoven's life was a witness that was forged in adversity and discouragement in times of desolation. It has been that way for The DeKoven Center as well. Not many years ago, the plans had actually been made to alter most of the historic buildings of The DeKoven Center, and even take over floors of Taylor Hall for condominiums. There were times when even the ministry of this holy and historic place was threatened. While I can't explain the mystery of desolation, I do believe the witness of James DeKoven and the witness of The DeKoven Center would somehow have been "less" without those times of discouragement. The outcry from the public and the marshaled efforts of countless community citizens to save DeKoven has also contributed to an extraordinary renewal of interest in the campus, its grounds, buildings, ministry, and community research.

The wonderful unfolding of ministry and fellowship at The DeKoven Center that we celebrate in this Sesquicentennial year was also forged in times of desolation. The darkness did not prevail in the life of James DeKoven, and the darkness did not prevail for the ministries of The DeKoven Center. The times of desolation have given way to times of consolation and growth. Those experiences provided the path for the ministry of The DeKoven Center as we know it today. So we need to remember the sacrifices and risks, the adventures in faith, and the efforts of local citizens that have made possible the celebration of this Sesquicentennial. This book contains a variety of essays to recall and celebrate the life of James DeKoven, as well as the evolving and developing ministries of The DeKoven Center.

James DeKoven knew that the fragments of life are all gathered into completion in Christ. May Christ continue to be known and engaged through the ministry of The DeKoven Center, for the next 150 years and beyond! And may this book help us always to remember the whole tradition and ministry that animate the life of The DeKoven Center.

Robert Boak Slocum
Co-Editor

CHAPTER 1

Biography of James DeKoven

Lawrence N. Crumb

James DeKoven was born on September 19, 1831, in Middletown, Connecticut. His father, Henry Louis DeKoven, was a banker whose assets were largely invested in land, including the early real estate of Chicago, where a street was named after him. His grandfather, Captain John Louis DeKoven (originally von Koven) had been brought over by the British to command a regiment of Hessian mercenaries during the Revolutionary War, but was captured in New York Bay and allowed to settle in Middletown. James's mother, Margaret Sebor, was her husband's cousin; their grandmother Sebor was a Winthrop, descended from two colonial governors of Massachusetts. By 1843, the family had moved to Brooklyn Heights, New York, where young James became active at Grace Church. He was the ninth of ten children; the oldest, Henry, was ordained in 1843 and later taught homiletics in the Berkeley Divinity School, then in Middletown. Henry's son, Reginald, was a successful composer whose works included the operetta *Robin Hood*, source of the long-popular song "Oh, Promise Me."

James DeKoven graduated from Columbia College in 1851, the second in his class; and from the General Theological Seminary in 1854, as valedictorian. His fellow-students at these institutions included the future bishops George Seymour (Springfield), John Brown (Fond du Lac), and Cyrus Knight (Milwaukee), and such other future clergy of distinction as Morgan Dix, who became rector of Trinity Church, Wall Street. During his seminary days, he helped to establish a "ragged school" for poor boys, in whom he took great interest. He was ordained deacon on August 6, 1854, in Middletown by Bishop Williams of Connecticut. Declining offers from two parishes, one of which was being started by the nearby parish where his older brother was rector, he arrived at Nashotah House on September 15 as professor of ecclesiastical history. This rural seminary, 30 miles west of Milwaukee, had been founded 12 years earlier as a mission center by three young men who had been, like DeKoven, high churchmen just out of the General Theological Seminary and not yet priests.

While at Nashotah, DeKoven was also rector of St. John Chrysostom, Delafield, often walking the two miles between the two posts. He was ordained to the priesthood there on September 23, 1855, by Bishop Kemper. Ten months earlier, he had opened a parish school on land adjacent to the church, where St. John's Military Academy now stands. In 1858, St. John's Hall, patterned after St. Peter's College, Radley, England, was opened as the preparatory

Rev. James De Koven D.D.

department for the seminary. At about this time, DeKoven visited England and France with his seminary roommate, George Seymour, later dean of the seminary and bishop of Springfield.

The nation-wide Panic of 1857-58 (as depressions were then called) led to the merger of St. John's Hall with Racine College in 1859, with DeKoven as Warden. It was on the Racine campus that he would spend the remaining twenty years of his life, building up both the physical plant and the spiritual life of the college. It had been founded in 1852 under the auspices of the diocese, but it was only loosely connected to the church. DeKoven quickly changed this situation, building a chapel that was the center of the college, both literally and figuratively. The chapel soon became noted (and, for some, notorious) for its "advanced" ritual practices. The student body grew to 220, a respectable number at the time. In 1875, the bishops of Colorado, Fond du Lac, Illinois, Indiana, Michigan, Missouri, Nebraska, Western Michigan, and Wisconsin adopted Racine College as their official college.

Meanwhile, DeKoven was gaining a national reputation as a leader of the ritualist party within the Episcopal Church. This made him a lightning rod for both accolades and attacks, the division of opinion beginning within his own diocese. In 1866, he was nominated as coadjutor to the aging Bishop Kemper but was defeated, partly by opposition from his former colleagues at Nashotah House. This can be explained only in part by the fact that his churchmanship was more "advanced" than theirs. No doubt, there was also some resentment over the continued devotion to him of many of the students who progressed from his college, still the seminary's preparatory department, to the seminary.

The Diocese of Milwaukee elected Dekoven as a deputy to General Convention in 1868, and every three years thereafter until his death. He became the spokesman for his party in the House of Deputies, and opposed the efforts to enact anti-ritual canons at the 1871 and 1874 General Conventions. In the former year, he was bold to state, "I believe in the Real, Actual Presence of Our Lord under the form of bread and wine upon the altars of our churches," admitting that adoration was the logical corollary to this doctrine. Although many of his fellow deputies disagreed violently with such sentiments, they respected the eloquence of his oratory and frequently granted him more time than normally allowed. But in resisting the proposed canons on ritual, he undermined his chance of ever becoming a bishop. In 1872, he narrowly missed election in the Diocese of Massachusetts; and in 1874, when the clergy of Wisconsin did elect him, the laity failed to concur. The latter election was especially bitter, with the clergy of Nashotah House (including Bishop Kemper's son) once again leading the opposition. The same division between clergy and laity occurred a year later in the new Diocese of Fond du Lac; and when, later that year, the Diocese of Illinois did elect him in both orders, he failed to receive the necessary consents from other dioceses. In the case of Illinois, DeKoven's personal unpopularity in certain circles was compounded by the fact that his election was widely seen as a slap in the face to the General Convention of 1874, which had refused to confirm the election by the Diocese of Illinois of his friend, Dean Seymour (who was confirmed as the first Bishop of Springfield in 1877, receiving his episcopal ring as a gift from DeKoven).

During his twenty years at Racine College, DeKoven received several offers of positions elsewhere: as rector of the Church of the Advent, Boston; of St. Mark's, Philadelphia; and of a parish in Cincinnati; also as assistant to his friend, Morgan Dix, at Trinity Church, New York, in a special position that would have been created for him. He replied to all these offers that he felt his duty was to his college. This does not mean that he had no outside interests other than his participation in General Convention. In 1878, he was instrumental in bringing the Community of St. Mary, the oldest existing religious order for women in the Episcopal Church, to assume the operation of Kemper Hall, a school for girls in nearby Kenosha. In his own city of Racine, he was involved in the founding of St. Luke's Hospital, Taylor Orphanage, and the Palmeter Home for elderly women. Within the diocese, he actively supported his bishop in his promotion of the "cathedral movement," the idea of a pastoral bishop in every large city, with a cathedral staff that could do things not possible in any one parish—a movement bitterly opposed by the cardinal rectors of Milwaukee, whose fear led them into a petty parochialism.

DeKoven's refusal of other positions may have derived, in part, from an awareness of his delicate health, although the less demanding position at Trinity Church in New York had been urged on him for that very reason. During his last several years, he had a nervous twitch in his arm and knew that he was threatened by apoplexy. Like the true saint, he did not seek death, but he was always ready for it. He looked forward to death with joy as the gate to a better life to which he would someday come, in God's good time. His last sermon, "The Victory of Faith," was preached at St. Paul's Cathedral, Fond du Lac, on January 26, 1879. In speaking of "true Christian hope," he proclaimed, "Death itself, with the darkness of its shadow, the coldness of its waves, the long, weary time of waiting which it brings, can never separate you from the love of Christ ..."

Father Robert Slocum of Lake Geneva and Father Travis Du Priest, director of The DeKoven Center, offer prayers at the Shrine of Blessed James DeKoven on DeKoven Day, March 22.

On March 19, the time of waiting ended, as death came to DeKoven in his bedroom at the college. He was recuperating from a broken ankle caused by a fall on the ice in Milwaukee four weeks earlier. A ritualist to the last, he was laid out in eucharistic vestments, with a crucifix on his breast. The funeral on March 22 was attended by the City Council as a body, the mayor having ordered all stores closed; the many clergy present included eight bishops. Three months later, a memorial cross was placed on the altar of his old church in Delafield, with the bishops of Missouri, Western Michigan, and Wisconsin in attendance. DeKoven's national reputation is most dramatically suggested by the unprecedented action of the General Convention which met in

Chicago in 1886: They declared a recess so that a large delegation, headed by eighteen bishops, could make a pilgrimage to DeKoven's grave on the Racine College campus. In 1963, the Standing Liturgical Commission of the Episcopal Church commemorated DeKoven on March 22 in a calendar of "Lesser Feasts and Fasts" approved for trial use by General Convention in the following year and included (with additions) in the 1979 Book of Common Prayer.

James DeKoven was many things: priest and preacher, educator and spiritual director, activist in church affairs and active observer of the secular sphere. He was, most obviously, an educator, from his deeply concerned involvement in the "ragged school" of his seminary days to his final will and testament, which left his library and small personal fortune to his beloved Racine College. Although not a scholar in the sense of one doing original research and publication, he was an outstanding student in both college and seminary, and received an appointment to teach in another seminary upon graduation. He was not only willing to operate a parish school at Delafield in addition to his other duties at seminary and parish, but he took delight in it, judging from this diary entry for November 15, 1854: "My Parish School opened today. Thank God! May He bless it and make it succeed!"

DeKoven became warden (i.e., president) of Racine College at 28, and received an honorary D.D. from Hobart College three years later. His friend Morgan Dix described him as having made a "fearless study of those old Catholic fathers, whom we are commanded by our Mother [church] to revere as our masters," and his understanding of Christian education placed as much emphasis on the adjective as on the noun. A professor who visited from Kenyon (like Hobart, an Episcopal Church-related college) remarked that he wished his school were like Racine's in every way except the chapel; DeKoven replied that Racine College without its chapel would be like Shakespeare's *Hamlet* without the title role. The description of Christmas festivities at the college, with the students still present, indicates that DeKoven, like William Augustus Muhlenberg at St. Paul's School on Long Island, considered the faculty and students to be a Christian community that needed to observe the major holy days together. The gentleness of his discipline reflected his general personality, and shows that he was a far cry from the typical caning headmaster of the day. His interest in education extended to his participation in the affairs of the national church. At the General Convention of 1868, he chaired the committee on Christian Education and obtained passage of a resolution recommending "the establishment of Christian schools, in every parish where it may be practicable."

DeKoven as priest is remembered for the care with which the services of the college chapel were celebrated. Although he was not a musician himself, he promoted the choral service, along with such ritual practices as vested choir, processional cross, and altar candles—all taken for granted today, but controversial at the time. He also heard the confessions of his students at the college. His theology and the content of his sermons are discussed elsewhere in this volume. Suffice it to say that his delivery was also noteworthy. He preached without notes, but not without preparation. Morgan Dix has left us an "ear-witness" description of "that wonderful voice, which, now ringing like a clarion, and anon sinking to the lowest, gentlest tones, thrilled the soul and sounded depths within men which perhaps in their case may never be touched again by mortal speech." In 1868, he preached before the Archbishop of Canterbury at St. Augustine's College in that city; and, in 1874, at Trinity Church, New York City.

The gentleness of DeKoven's personality has already been mentioned. Another dimension is revealed by his writing a hymn at age twelve and a small book of poems at fifteen. His book, *The Dorchester Polytechnic Academy,* consisted of imaginative stories he told to the Racine College students on Sunday afternoons. Although a lifelong celibate, he was a gracious host to visitors of both sexes and arranged for one of his sisters to live at the college. Uncompromising in his principles, he was a man strongly liked by some and strongly disliked by others. Mary Todd Lincoln described him as a "suave cassocked Jesuit." The city of Racine named the northern boundary of the college DeKoven Avenue during his lifetime, and turned out in great numbers for his funeral.

A man noted for his spirituality, DeKoven was also very practical and wise in the ways of the world. He went to Racine in 1859 as part of an academic merger made necessary by the nation-wide depression of that year. He proved an able fund-raiser for the college. He came from a commercial family, and when he preached against the materialism of the age, he was able to speak with knowledge of mining and farming, of real estate speculation and the building of railroads. He was also aware of a changing intellectual climate, and remarked in one sermon that "the miracles of one age become the science of another."

The breadth of DeKoven's many qualities is indicated by these words from a memorial sermon by his close friend, The Rev. Clinton Locke, rector of Grace Church, Chicago: "Dr. DeKoven was not only one of the most brilliant orators, one of the finest scholars, one of the most clear debaters in the Church, but he was one of the holiest, one of the saintliest of all her sons. His life was lived upon a very lofty plane, far above the ordinary level.

"DeKoven was not an ascetic; he was not gloomy, but he conveyed even to the chance observer the impression of great personal holiness. He spent hours upon his knees, and from his childhood to his grave he was singularly free from even what are called venial sins. But with this very holy and pure life there was no spiritual pride, no assumption of superior worthiness. When you add to all this a thoroughly charming manner, a perfect culture, an intimate knowledge of all the graces of polite society, and a personal magnetism which gave him wonderful power over the young men under his care, who without exception idolized him, the greatness of the loss is overpowering."

Many years later, DeKoven's greatness was expressed more succinctly by The Rev. Walter C.

Klein, assistant dean of Seabury-Western Theological Seminary and later dean of Nashotah House and Bishop of Northern Indiana. Preaching at the DeKoven Day ceremonies of 1958, he proclaimed, "I have no hesitation in saying, 'Blessed James DeKoven, pray for us.'"

SOURCES

Chorley, E. Clowes. "The Anglo-Catholic Movement." In his *Men and Movements in the American Episcopal Church*. The Hale Lectures. New York: Charles Scribner's Sons, 1946. 315-58 (322-34 for DeKoven).

Crumb, Lawrence N. "Religion." In *Racine: Growth and Change in a Wisconsin County*. Ed. Nicholas C. Burckel. Racine, Wis.: Racine County Board of Supervisors, 1977. 487-542, 599-613 (523-24 for DeKoven).

DeKoven, Anna [Mrs. Reginald]. "Marriage." In her *A Musician and His Wife*. New York and London: Harper & Brothers, 1926. 83-96 (85-96 for family background).

"DeKoven, James." *Appleton's Cyclopaedia of American Biography*. New York: Appleton, 1887-1924. 2:126.

DeMille, George E. *The Catholic Movement in the American Episcopal Church*. Publication 12. Philadelphia: Church Historical Society, 1941. *passim* (see Index).

Dix, Morgan. "Preface." In *Sermons Preached on Various Occasions*. By James DeKoven. New York: D. Appleton, and Co., 1880. iii-xvii.

Gallagher, Katharine Jeanne. "DeKoven, James." *Dictionary of American Biography*. New York, Charles Scribner's Sons, 1928-58. 3:205-06.

McElroy, Gary A. "James DeKoven and the Wisconsin Election of 1874." *American Church Quarterly* 4, no. 3 (Fall 1964): 182-96.

Morehouse, Frederic Cook. "James DeKoven, Warden of Racine College." In *Some American Churchmen*. Milwaukee: The Young Churchman Co., 1892. 157-234.

Pope, William C. *Life of the Reverend James DeKoven, D.D., Sometime Warden of Racine College.* New York: James Pott & Co., 1899.

Reeves, Thomas C. "DeKoven, James." *American National Biography.* New York: Oxford University Press, 1999. 6:358-59.

Reeves, Thomas C., Ed. *James DeKoven, Anglican Saint.* Racine, Wis.: DeKoven Foundation for Church Work, 1978. (Sermons by DeKoven.)

"Was James DeKoven a Saint?" By a Sister of Saint Mary. *Living Church* 139, no. 15 (October 11, 1959): 12-13, 18.

CHAPTER 2

Romantic Religion and the Witness of James DeKoven[1]

Robert Boak Slocum

Romantic religion in the nineteenth century was characterized by its appreciation for symbol and mystery. Romantic religion was idealistic. It found value in human experience and inner feelings. At times the romantic gospel served as "a specific prescription for the spiritual paralysis brought on by a diet of common-sense rationalism."[2] Romantic religion upheld the continuity of community and tradition in the face of a critical rationality that often seemed coldly logical in application. Romantic theology conveyed a sense of "the infinite beyond" relative to the finite and concrete, the "paltry this-and-that" of existence.[3] It pointed to the transcendent, countering the emphasis on empiricism that dominated eighteenth century philosophy.

Such romantic themes were evident in the work of James DeKoven, an Episcopal priest who served in Wisconsin during the latter part of the nineteenth century. He was at the center of controversies that swirled around the catholic movement in the Episcopal Church of his time. He cannot be dismissed or entirely summed up with a term such as "romantic." His faith was in Jesus Christ, and not merely the result of a tendency or style that was in vogue during his time. But the language, the emphases, and the concerns of his work reflected the romantic religion of his era.

James DeKoven (1831-1879) is commemorated in the Episcopal Calendar of the Church year on March 22. He attended the General Theological Seminary, which was at the time a "national center of High Churchmanship...with roots in the teachings of American Bishops Samuel Seabury and John Henry Hobart and in the Church of England's Oxford Movement."[4] Thomas C. Reeves notes that DeKoven emerged from General Seminary as "an advanced High Churchman, or ritualist, uncompromisingly committed to Catholic liturgy, ceremonial and architecture."[5]

After seminary DeKoven accepted the chair of ecclesiastical history at Nashotah House, a seminary and mission center that was west of Milwaukee in rural Wisconsin. The founders of Nashotah House had intended to give it "more or less of a monastic character," and it was "organized under definitely Anglo-Catholic auspices."[6] DeKoven was understandably drawn to Nashotah House. He also served as Rector of the Church of St. John Chrysostom in nearby Delafield, and Warden of St. John's Hall, a preparatory school for boys. St. John's Hall was designed to prepare students for Nashotah House.

St. John's Chapel, The DeKoven Center

DeKoven began his life's work as Warden of Racine College when St. John's Hall merged with the Racine school in 1859. He was twenty-eight years old at the time. He served there until his death.

DeKoven's leadership at Racine College reflected his dedication to liturgy, ceremonial and sacraments. There were two chapel services daily, including evensong with a vested student choir.[7] The Racine College choir was put in surplices in 1865.[8] He trained his students to make their confessions, and he once heard between fifty and sixty confessions during Holy Week.[9] The first choral Eucharist was held at Racine College in 1866, and a daily Eucharist became the rule in 1876.[10] These practices were very "advanced" for the time.

DeKoven was best known for his defense of eucharistic adoration at the General Conventions of 1871 and 1874, where he was the "leader of the High Church forces" in the House of Deputies.[11] The 1871 debate on ritual has been termed "one of the greatest debates in the history of the General Convention," with DeKoven leading the opposition to the proposed canon on ritual.[12] He urged that such practices as altar lights, genuflections, and the use of incense "symbolize the real, spiritual presence of Christ" and do not symbolize the doctrine of transubstantiation. DeKoven supported this argument by an appeal to tradition and to the customs of other liturgical churches. He noted that such practices preceded the doctrine of transubstantiation, and were used in Lutheran and Orthodox churches which also repudiated transubstantiation.[13]

DeKoven appealed for comprehensiveness and tolerance in worship. William Manross noted that his speech at the 1874 General Convention "put the argument upon an entirely new basis," which was a departure from the tendency of both sides up to that point "to seek the greatest possible restraint upon their opponents."[14] Manross noted that in 1871 DeKoven "was the only avowed ritualist in the House of Deputies, and probably the only really brilliant orator that House ever produced."[15]

Despite his losing part of the canonical battle at the 1874 General Convention, it was DeKoven's vision of a comprehensive approach to worship that ultimately prevailed in the Episcopal Church. But his appreciation of sacramental mystery was costly for him. His forceful advocacy of the ritualist cause at the 1871 and 1874 General Conventions also called into question his views of the Eucharist in some quarters of the Episcopal Church, and "killed DeKoven's chances of a bishopric."[16] DeKoven narrowly missed episcopal election in the Diocese of Massachusetts in 1873, and in the Diocese of Fond du Lac in 1874. His views on ritual and belief were challenged when he was nominated to be Bishop of Wisconsin in 1874. The controversy became so intense that he took the floor to defend himself at diocesan convention. He later withdrew from the election in the Diocese of Wisconsin. DeKoven was elected Bishop of Illinois in 1875, but his election was not approved by the necessary number of standing committees in the other dioceses of the Episcopal Church.

DeKoven's romanticism is suggested by George E. DeMille, who observed that "A reading of his single volume of published sermons, with their intense mystical note, their warmth of personal devotion to our Lord and to the sacrament of the altar, shows plainly how far this generation had advanced from the sometimes pedantic dogmatism of some of the older school of High Churchmen."[17] The romantic tendency of DeKoven's beliefs and practice is reflected in his "devotion to the sacraments, his desire to beautify church services with altar lights, incense, flowers, crosses, ornate vestments and the like, plus his missionary zeal," which "placed him throughout his lifetime within a minority of his priestly peers."[18] His romantic religion, especially as revealed in his published sermons and diary, is considered in the following discussion in terms of various romantic themes or tendencies in his work.

The Limits of Reason

DeKoven upheld the supernatural and mysterious dimension of faith. In the sermon "The Fullness of Joy," he warned, "Once lose the idea of the Divine indwelling, once fritter it away by rationalistic explanations, even make it less than it is, and a blow is struck at civilization, at the advancement of the human race...."[19] He pointed out the limits of reason in matters of faith. He stated in the sermon "The Gates of the Invisible" that he did "not wish to undervalue the use of reason, or the value of evidences, or the mighty power of the proofs of Christianity. I only wish to put them in their true position; they rather serve to confirm the faith than to proclaim it."[20] As an example of the limits of reason, DeKoven considered the human soul. He noted that the soul cannot be discovered by the knife of an anatomist or found in the folds of the brain. "And yet it needs no proof; it has not to be argued about; it admits of no denial. It is, and we know it is."[21] He identified a spiritual dimension of human life that exceeds empirical data or pure reason.

DeKoven saw rationalism in the American

culture around him, and he opposed the hesitancy that this spirit of rationality seemed to cause in those who should be willing to share the mysteries of faith. In the sermon "The Dead in Christ," he noted that the American people are an "intensely real and practical people," and asked, "What [is] more in opposition to their views and feelings than the invisible, the supernatural, the mystical, the awful verities of the unseen?"[22]

Because of this lack of appreciation for the supernatural and mystical, DeKoven warned, "Churchmen have too often, instead of presenting the blessed truths which are really needed to counteract the tendencies and meet the real wants of the people, presented the awful mysteries of the Faith, with an apology and an explanation which too often explained them away."[23] He also noted the irony that "real and practical people, who deny the invisible and reject the spiritual" are deceived by superstitious and bogus spiritualism "which transforms the blessed communion that exists between the living and the death in the Catholic Church into the communications which pretend to come from the souls of the departed."[24] He blamed the spread of this error on the Church's reluctance to preach the supernatural and traditional doctrine of the communion of saints.

DeKoven also underscored the traditional importance of episcopal ministry. There was no Anglican bishop in the American colonies or the Episcopal Church until 1784, over 177 years after the first Anglican celebration of the Eucharist in Virginia in 1607. He blamed a number of ills in the Church on this delay in the advent of episcopal leadership, including the rationalistic and untraditional tendencies of the proposed prayer book in 1786. In the sermon "In Loving Memory," DeKoven asked, rhetorically,

> Was it wonderful that the Prayer Book proposed at such a time, but rejected, should have embodied the rationalism and indifferentism and lurking Socialism of an evil time? Ought we to be surprised that it should have left out the Creed of universal Christendom and mutilated the Apostles Creed; that it should have denied the grace of Holy Baptism, and in the interest of latitudinarians cut out from its Articles the chief protests against Roman error?[25]

DeKoven's contradiction of "rationalism and indifferentism" in the Church and the world reflected his romantic impatience with pure reason in matters of faith and his dedication to the traditional and the mysterious.

Natural and Supernatural

Another aspect of DeKoven's romantic religion was his discernment of the interpenetration of the natural and supernatural orders, with the supernatural order hidden but yet perceptible in its glory. In his letter to the convention of the Diocese of Illinois, he defended eucharistic adoration in terms of this interpenetration of natural and supernatural:

> .... if the spiritual and material worlds are, so to speak, interlaced; if were our eyes only opened we could see the 'horses and chariots of

fire round about Elisha,' and were our ears rightly tuned, we could hear celestial harmonies; if the sacraments were the doors of entrance into this spiritual world, then might it be conceived that the presence of Christ at the right hand of the Father, and His sacramental presence in the Eucharist are one and the same, and the adoration given to the one is adoration given to the other....[26]

This vivid perception of transcendent glory in the midst of the natural order also gives a larger perspective to the events and occasions of everyday life—including natural beauty and individual success. In the sermon "Treasures New and Old," DeKoven reflected both a romantic appreciation for natural beauty and a devotion to God's unseen and surpassing glory. He urged that:

> To realize beauty, to love art, to appreciate nature, to be sensitive to color and form and sound, to vibrate, like the strings of an Aeolian harp, to all the hidden harmonies of the summer air, and yet to surrender all these, or to use them sparingly for the sake of strength and power and higher good... this is to be like Him who, though he was rich, yet for our sakes became poor....[27]

DeKoven found the visible to be surrounded by the invisible, and the natural overarched by the supernatural. Nature is a wonder to be appreciated and treasured, he noted, but there is a higher good for the devotion of the faithful.

In concluding his last sermon, "The Victory of Faith," DeKoven explained the perspective given by the interpenetration of natural and supernatural in light of the "victory of faith":

Rock garden of The Bishop's Garden at The DeKoven Center

To surrender the will, to humble the pride, to become like a little child; to believe in the unseen; to know that there is another world than that about us, to enter it by Baptism, to live in it by the Holy Communion; to be guided by the voice and hand of an invisible Master; to be drawn nearer and nearer to that blessed Home of which death is only the portal; to see the solemn pageant of the world's great activities go marching by as in a spectacle; to be in it, yet far above it; to despise none of its beauty or goodness or excellence, and yet to have the life hid with Christ in God; above its din and noise, to hear celestial harmonies; in the midst of its hurry and bustle, to be at peace; to care neither for its honors nor its persecutions; sober in prosperity, patient and resigned in adversity, at rest in life, at rest in death, one with Christ for ever—this is the victory that overcometh the world, even our faith![28]

Fullness of Worship

DeKoven's romantic religion included special appreciation for the places and forms of sacred worship. The place of worship should be no barren meeting hall; the Church's words and expressions of worship provide much more than rational edification. He noted, "The house of God and its blessed services are the place and the manner whereby we approach the awe-inspiring presence of the King of kings...."[29] DeKoven's romantic spirit was evident in his description of a funeral procession at Racine College after the death of a student. He recalled in his diary:

> The boys were waiting drawn up in long array and in front the white robed choristers. The evening was very beautiful, the western sky was all aglow with rosy light. The Lake lay to the east of the road, calm and placid as though appeased, and in the east the moon shed that half light which is so beautiful before the day vanishes. On moved the procession. They sang 'Have mercy upon me, O God, after thy great goodness' and then 'Out of the deep,' and as they entered the graveyard, sweetly in harmony, 'The Lord is my Shepherd.' The daylight faded more and more, the surpliced boys in the pale moonlight seemed to lose their earthliness and to resemble the white robed ones above, and as they sang at the close of all from memory 'Softly now the light of day,' it seemed beautiful and peaceful beyond all words.[30]

Many elements made up this vivid scene for DeKoven—the white vestments of the students in procession, the natural beauty of the lakefront

Vested choir boys on steps of St. John's Chapel

setting at twilight, the hymns of peace and hope that evoked in him a hushed and devout religious feeling.

Similarly, he recounted in his diary the time when he found a student playing the melodeon at night in the Racine College Chapel:

> ... there was a faint gleam from the Chapel windows. I went to the Chapel. Quite alone at the melodeon practicing his music sat Edward. There was just enough light to lighten up the part around him, but the shadows were dark and heavy a little distance away. It pleased me to see him thus alone in the Chapel. Perhaps the shadow of the great cross over the rood screen fell upon him. Who knows what sweet thoughts the blessed Angels which guard the altar may have put into his heart. It may be the Unseen Presence of Him Whose House it is which came nearer and nearer to him. Perhaps the imperfect melodies he made were made full of deepest harmony by his Guardian Angel and wafted upward.[31]

This scene also discloses DeKoven's sensitivity to God's unseen presence in the midst of the shadows and symbols of worship and the "imperfect melodies" of the student practicing in the chapel. The chapel, he felt, was a holy place, filled with the presence of God and angelic guardians, where visitors might be drawn to greater devotion and deeper communion with God.

Faith of the Heart and Personal Conversion

DeKoven's romantic religion was a religion of the heart, not limited to rationality. His theology was catholic in its appreciation of tradition, sacrament, and symbol. It was also evangelical in its appeal for personal conversion and a response of the believer's heart to God's offer of salvation. DeKoven's faith was deeply felt, and he sought to reach the feelings of others. In his Ash Wednesday sermon "The Gates of the Invisible," he asked:

> Is there one in this congregation who does not know that at some time or another, once or twice or more—when I cannot tell, but he knows—Christ has stood by him? Did He not call to you? Did He not speak to you? Did He not plead with you? Did He not show you His wounded hands?.... Was it when you were sick? Was it when you were bidden to Confirmation? Was it before the altar when the Mystical Presence flashed upon you? Was it in the stillness of the night, or at some time when nothing masked it except that He was there? Is it *now*, perhaps, my child—on this Ash Wednesday—as this Lent begins?[32]

His appeal for personal conversion and response of faith is deeply rooted in the seasons and the sacraments of the Church. In his sermon "Gathering Up the Fragments" on the Last Sunday after Trinity, DeKoven warned, "Perhaps it is your last Church year. Before another Advent, with its winter cold, and its solemn words, shall be here, you may rest in death. It can not be for ever. The last Church service must come, the last warning words be heard, the last prayers sound on the ear, the last invitation to the Holy Communion be given."[33] But he continued: "the Gospel for the day tells of something still that can be done, even for a wasted life, saying, 'Gather up the fragments that remain, that nothing be lost.' The fragments of a life, beloved! The broken pieces of a mighty whole—they may be gathered up again."[34]

DeKoven offered hope for the penitent who has wasted much, especially the one who will receive God's gift of salvation as the new Church year and the season of Advent draw near. He made an ardent promise:

> What is gone may yet be recovered: you may redeem the time. Only follow your Master to the wilderness if need be. Be hungry and thirsty after righteousness. Let Him feed you. Then, as the years go by, and the flowers fade, and the leaves fall withered and sere, the sound of the Advent trump, come as it will, will be as welcome as the first light of the morning to the weary watcher, or as tidings from home to the captive exile.[35]

Pious practices were commended by DeKoven as aids to conversion, including the traditional exercises and devotions. In his Ash Wednesday sermon "The Gates of the Invisible," he considered the possibility that one may be unable to see Christ because "Sin, and pleasure, and self-indulgence, and want of prayer, or some dark deed have driven Him away." He continued:

> I answer then, it was for this that the Church appointed the Lenten season. Faith, and prayer, and fasting, and tears, and self-denial, and confession, and kneeling in His courts—these are the Gates of the Invisible. Once, with His help, open them, and within, patient and loving still, your Lord will stand.[36]

DeKoven's appeal for a change of heart also pointed beyond the selfishness he found in the world around him. His idealism was evident in his discussion of loyalty in the sermon "Gathering Up the Fragments":

> O my friend! Be loyal to something, not yourself; to an abstraction, an idea, a notion, if you can do no better; to your father and mother, to your friend or your teacher, to the woman you love, to a priest or a statesman, to the man who embodies some great cause and suffers for it! Forget yourself and your own interest, your faults, your sins, your virtues, your wants, your hopes, your fears, and find in this forgetfulness of self a deeper knowledge, a purer aim, a *more enduring reward*.[37]

He reminded his hearers that there is much more in life than reasonable, enlightened self-interest.

DeKoven's appeal for conversion of heart was evangelical in its fervor, and based on the traditions, seasons, and symbols of the Church. He sought to kindle the feelings of his hearers with a new

St. John's Chapel, March 22, 1879, the day of Blessed Father James DeKoven's funeral.

enthusiasm of faith. He was sensitive to the beauty of nature and art, especially the beauty of the Church's liturgies and places of worship. DeKoven was responsive to the mystery and power of God's unseen presence that can transform individual lives.

END NOTES

[1] Reprinted with permission from *Anglican and Episcopal History/The Historical Magazine of the Protestant Episcopal Church*, LXV: 1 (March, 1996), 82-111.

[2] Sydney E. Ahlstrom, *A Religious History of the American People* (New Haven, 1972), 599. Ahlstrom makes this comment in a chapter on "Romantic Religion in New England."

[3] Bernard M. G. Reardon, *Religion in the Age of Romanticism, Studies in Early Nineteenth Century Thought* (Cambridge, 1985), 3.

[4] Thomas C. Reeves, "Introduction," in *James DeKoven, Anglican Saint*, ed., Thomas Reeves (Racine, 1978), 2.

[5] *Ibid.*

[6] William Wilson Manross, *A History of the American Episcopal Church* (New York, 1935), 275.

[7] Reeves, Introduction, 2.

[8] E. Clowes Chorley, *Men and Movements in the American Episcopal Church* (New York, 1948), 325.

[9] *Ibid.*

[10] *Ibid.*, 325-326.

[11] George E. DeMille, *The Catholic Movement in the American Episcopal Church, Second Edition, Revised and Enlarged* (New Brunswick, New Jersey, 1950), 93.

[12] Chorley, *Men and Movements*, 382.

[13] *Ibid.*

[14] Manross, *American Episcopal Church*, 300.

[15] *Ibid.*, 297-298.

[16] DeMille, *Catholic Movement*, 119. Although DeMille makes this comment with respect to DeKoven's speech at the 1871 General Convention, it holds equally true with respect to the whole of DeKoven's advocacy against a canon on ritual.

[17] *Ibid.*, 94.

[18] Reeves, Introduction, 2. Reeves notes that many of DeKoven's beliefs are now "commonplace in the Church."

[19] James DeKoven, *Sermons Preached on Various Occasions* (New York, 1880), 139. ["The Fullness of Joy," preached at Convocation, Milwaukee, 1872.]

[20] *Ibid.*, 160. ["The Gates of the Invisible," preached at Racine College, Ash Wednesday, 1878.]

[21] *Ibid.*

[22] *Ibid.*, 69. ["The Dead in Christ," preached at St. Stephen's College, Annandale, All Saints' Day, 1866.]

[23] *Ibid.*

[24] *Ibid.*, 70.

[25] *Ibid.*, 238. ["In Loving Memory," preached in All Saints' Cathedral, Milwaukee, February 10, 1874, after the death of The Rt. Rev. William Edmond Armitage, Bishop of Milwaukee.]

[26] James DeKoven, *A Letter from The Rev. James DeKoven, D.D., Warden of Racine College, to the Clergy and Laity of the Diocese of Illinois, in Convention Assembled, September 14, 15, 16, 17, A.D. 1875. Together with the Action of the Convention of the Diocese of Illinois Thereon* (Chicago, 1875), 9-10.

[27] DeKoven, *Sermons*, 330. ["Treasures New and Old," preached at Racine College Commencement, June, 1878, Baccalaureate Sermon.]

[28] *Ibid.*, 363-364. ["The Victory of Faith," preached at Fond du Lac, January 26, 1879.]

[29] *Ibid.*, 70. ["The Dead in Christ."]

[30] James DeKoven, *DeKoven Diary* (Unpublished manuscript in the collection of the DeKoven Center, Racine, Wisconsin), 46.

[31] *Ibid.*, 50. "Edward" was Edward Larrabee, who later became an Episcopal priest and Dean of Nashotah House Seminary. See Chorley, 325, n. 19.

[32] DeKoven, *Sermons*, 163. ["The Gates of the Invisible."]

[33] *Ibid.*, 314. ["Gathering Up the Fragments," preached at Racine College, the Last Sunday after Trinity, 1878.] The sermon was preached within four months of DeKoven's death.

[34] *Ibid.*, 315. The Gospel text for the sermon was John 6:12.

[35] *Ibid.*, 319.

[36] *Ibid.*, 163. ["The Gates of the Invisible."]

[37] *Ibid.*, 331. ["Gathering Up the Fragments."]

CHAPTER 3

James DeKoven, Novelist:
A Review of *Dorchester Polytechnic Academy; Dr. Neverasole, Principal*

Mabel Benson Du Priest

According to the brief preface that accompanies the 1879 publication of Dr. DeKoven's only known novel, the story has its origins in his custom of entertaining "his boys" by his own story-telling. It is useful to keep this venue in mind: a group of youngsters gathered together in front of a fireplace on a snowy winter's evening, as their Warden spins a tale of humor and instruction, with clear portraits of virtue and vice, creating just enough suspense to cause his listeners to fear for the hero's outcome, but not so much that his vindication is ever in serious doubt. A tale designed, following the dictum of Horace, "to teach and delight."

Dorchester Polytechnic Academy can be read from a variety of perspectives. It may be read primarily as a period piece; or it may be of interest simply because of its author. As the preface indicates, it is "so very different from any of his other publications," and thus, those persons who know Dr. DeKoven as a theologian may be intrigued by this other aspect of his writings. It may, of course, be read simply as novel, and evaluated on its literary merit. While the first two perspectives would probably lead to a sympathetic reading, the third perspective is more challenging.

For a modern reader, certain aspects of the novel are problematic because the teaching is so overt. The plot of the novel is a standard cautionary tale: a depiction of a virtuous life, and depictions of various deviations from virtue, and the consequences of each. The main character, Robert Graham, has been raised under the precepts of his saintly grandmother, and when he becomes the ward of his uncle and is enrolled in Dorchester Polytechnic Academy, he continues to live by those precepts. At first he is a curiosity and even an object of derision to some of the other boys, but by the end of the novel, his virtue is vindicated and he becomes a hero among them.

The action of the novel grows out of a scheme developed by an older boy named Durkey. This boy masterminds a theft from Mr. Whooney, one of the masters, and then cleverly manipulates the evidence to make it appear that Robert has stolen the money. In the climax of the novel, Robert is faced with two choices: he may admit to the theft and agree to its repayment, a choice that will result in his suffering no real consequences; or he may persist in his claim of innocence. In choosing to do this he can expect to be dismissed from school, arrested, and tried as a thief.

The pattern of a conflict and a choice is standard for a cautionary tale, but in Dr. DeKoven's novel the pattern is made more sophisticated than might be expected in a tale designed only to instruct boys. A more obvious moralistic tale, especially one devised by a warden or headmaster, might be a story the point of which would be to emphasize the virtue of confessing to a misdeed. Here, however, the virtue is maintaining the truth, persevering in declaring innocence, and the moral context involves not only Robert but those who judge his guilt or innocence. In this focusing of the moral context, the cautionary tale told by Dr. DeKoven might well be as much self-directed as it is directed to his listeners.

We see this self-admonition in the passage that describes Robert's encounter with his grandmother. Because he is believed to be a thief, Robert has been sent home from school. When he reaches home, his grandmother, who is near death, exhorts him to confess his wrongdoing, if he is guilty. The description of Robert's response may perhaps be drawn from Dr. DeKoven's own experience: In asserting his innocence—"'Grandmother, I did not do it,'" Robert "fixed upon her that look which none but the innocent can give—a look which, when once seen on the face of a child, can never be mistaken by any one, who has the heart to read it aright" (173). A reader wonders if this episode has its basis in Dr. DeKoven's own experience, the lesson being that detecting guilt in an offender is perhaps relatively easy in comparison to detecting innocence, though the latter may be even more important; and, in addition, that the skill to read such an expression "aright" is—for a person entrusted with task of judging a child's guilt or innocence—a moral obligation. A detail like this, revealing such self-perception and such a sense of obligation to the children in his charge, goes far to explain the affection Dr. DeKoven evoked in the boys at Racine College.

The problem with Robert, as a literary creation, is that he is too good to be true. Of course, Dr. DeKoven is not the only writer whose challenge is to make a virtuous character interesting. As we know, in every century since it was written, readers of Milton's *Paradise Lost* have preferred Satan to Christ as a literary character. But if the novel is placed in a different literary context, the expectations for Robert change. The novel can be read not only as a cautionary tale, but also as an example of the morality genre, in which forces of good and evil compete for the soul of an "Everyman" character.

From the perspective of this genre, Robert becomes the "Good Angel" figure, placed in opposition to the forces of evil: Durkey, specifically, but in general the whole moral framework of Dorchester Polytechnic Academy. As the "Good Angel" figure, his perseverance in virtue is never seriously in doubt and thus his static quality is appropriate. In this reading, the "Everyman" figure, the character who has the capacity to rise or fall on the moral ladder, is represented by some particular boys at the school; and even, in one especially interesting episode,

Dr. Neverasole himself. Thus, while he may not become more interesting as a literary character, at least Robert's one-dimensional nature has a rationale; it is no more than what would be expected from a character fulfilling the morality role of Goodness.

An additional demonstration of the novel's similarity to the morality tradition appears in an episode near the end of the novel, an episode in which Dr. Neverasole travels to Dorchester on what he expects to be an ordinary business trip. What happens, however, is a series of encounters which significantly effect Dr. Neverasole. First he encounters a former student who, according to the values of the academy, had been a star pupil. But now, as he confesses to Dr. Neverasole, he has become a defaulter, and intends to flee his obligations and escape to Europe. He no sooner has assured Dr. Neverasole that despite his guilt he has no worries about the world to come, thanks to the teachings of the Universalists, than he is suddenly killed as he steps off the train.

In the next encounter, another former student declares himself so addicted to dissipations that he expects they will shortly kill him. When Dr. Neverasole finally arrives in Dorchester, considerably shaken, he finds himself involved, unintentionally and almost against his will, in a funeral that he eventually learns is for the very man he has come to see. This chapter reads very much like a conventional feature of the morality, that being The Coming of Death, in which the Everyman figure is warned of his own mortality. Like an Everyman figure, Dr. Neverasole is strongly effected by his experience, and it prepares the way for his "conversion" in the last scene.

Whether or not Dr. DeKoven had the morality genre in mind as he constructed the novel can be only conjectured, but in any event it is not the only literary influence that can be detected in the novel. Traces of two other literary models can be seen, those being works by his own near contemporaries, Nathaniel Hawthorne and Herman Melville. The episode of Dr. Neverasole in Dorchester—the progress of the episode from one strange encounter to another, the use of procession, the surrealistic quality of the events, and the effect of the experience on a main character—these qualities are strongly reminiscent of what occurs in Hawthorne's short story "My Kinsman Major Molineaux" when the young protagonist of that tale, Robin, goes to Boston to find his kinsman.

Another literary analog can be seen in the main character, Robert, whose situation is very like the protagonist of Melville's *Billy Budd*. Robert, like Billy, represents good in conflict with evil, an evil seemingly motivated simply by the presence of the good. In both works the hero suffers undeservedly, but in this novel he is saved. In the last scene, a former student's death-bed confession implicates the real thief and vindicates Robert.

It is scenes such as this, and the earlier death-bed scene of one of the school boys, that provide the sentimental quality of the novel, a quality so much appreciated in the nineteenth century, and so disliked in our own. Also working against appreciation of the novel as a piece of literature is Dr.

DeKoven's fondness for the "deus ex machina" motif. In a number of instances Robert hears, as it were, a voice from heaven, as a scriptural passage comes to mind. Similarly troublesome to readers who desire verisimilitude are the several occasions when a beam of light, like a divine finger pointing, shines in on the hero's face. These, along with the overt "sermons" that occur from time to time, keep the novel from achieving significance as a piece of literature.

Nevertheless, there is great enjoyment to be found here, enjoyment, that in my opinion overbalances the flaws, which are perhaps unavoidable given the author's purpose and audience. The enjoyment comes from Dr. DeKoven's talent for entertaining. He may be teaching timeless lessons in a now less-than-palatable method, but any reader, in his century or ours, will enjoy and appreciate his skill as a comic writer, his ability to create comic characters and comic scenes, and to create biting, recognizable, and laugh-inducing satire.

First his comic characters, chief of whom is Mrs. Jollipop, the matron of the academy, and its only positive feature. She is a Dickens-like character, the servant who provides whatever creature comforts and mothering the boys at the school might receive. She is also a moral ballast; her instinctive good moral judgment is made clear in her opening appearance, when at first glance she approves of Robert and when she also makes it clear she has judged Durkey correctly: "'If he ain't the 'pomps and vanities of this wicked world, and all the sinful lusts of the flesh,' then my name isn't Betsey Jollipop!'" (44) she exclaims. It is clear from this that her instinctive good sense can separate the good from the evil, and that she can see through the facade of Durkey while the supposedly more experienced and sophisticated Dr. Neverasole is completely taken in.

Mrs. Jollipop figures in a number of comic episodes, one of which being the letter she writes which she hopes will support Robert's innocence (she is his one true supporter at the school). The intention of the letter is to confirm that the gold pieces Robert has been seen to have were given him by his old nurse Mrs. Dorothy. The letter Mrs. Jollipop writes moves by stream of consciousness from her health, to the price of pickles, to the high prices generally because of the war, to her experience with "colored" servants, to a recipe for sausages, never once mentioning the money. When this is eventually pointed out to her, a postcript is added, as comic as the letter itself.

The scene in which her good-natured but misguided qualities are best shown, however, is her encounter, along with Dr. Neverasole's daughter Mehitabel (called Hetty), with the wife of the Bishop of Dorchester and a young woman named Lucy. This scene is related to the sub-plot of the novel, the love interest between Mr. Whooney (the victim of the theft), and his sweetheart, who remained behind in England while he came to America to earn money. Now Lucy has inherited a sum that will make their marriage possible, and Mrs. Bishop (as she is called) brings her to the academy to help re-unite her with her intended. Mrs. Jollipop had heard Mr. Whooney talk about Lucy, but doesn't like her. She thought

Lucy's being a daughter of a minor canon had something to do with gunpowder. Also, from the picture Mr. Whooney has shown her, she thinks Lucy is ugly; and so, taking all things together it is her opinion Hetty Neverasole would be a much better choice. All that changes when Lucy and Mrs. Bishop appear at her door.

Mrs. Jollipop is overcome by the presence of a Bishop's wife ("a Bishop, in Mrs. Jollipop's mind, came next in order to the angels, and a Bishop's wife was almost as exalted"[166]). She gets it into her head that Mrs. Bishop has come "armed with all sorts of canons and ecclesiastical terrors" (166) and thinks somehow that the conversation has an ecclesiastical purpose. No matter how straightforwardly Mrs. Bishop asks her questions: who are you, where is Mr. Whoony?—Mrs. Jollipop responds from the Prayer Book as if she is being examined for confirmation, and insists that Hetty—whom she has pulled into the room with her—do the same, until finally the Bishop's dumbfounded wife concludes that they must both be crazy.

Other modes of humor seen in the novel are irony and satire. Sometimes the irony is obvious sarcasm, as in the repeated use of the adjective "excellent" in relation to Dr. Neverasole. Sometimes, in reference to other denominations such as the Universalist church, or Harvard Divinity School, it seems heavy-handed. Satire is used more effectively because it is used internally, in self-critique. Among the fullest and most enjoyable satirical developments are the depictions of the Episcopal clergy of Dorchester. In these sections, readers contemporary with

Dr. DeKoven would easily have recognized the satiric portraits, but even after the passage of time, readers with some knowledge of different theological perspectives can enjoy the humor.

The satire not only distinguishes various religious perspectives among the clergy, but also conveys the contrast between the status of the clergy and the episcopate—the episcopate in this case represented by the Bishop of Dorchester, whose small house was dwarfed by the impressive parsonage of one of his clergy. The clergy of the town seem to have replaced the Bishop in terms of significance, at least in terms of outward importance. There were "four Episcopal Rectors, who were really the Bishops of Dorchester. Dr. Gooby was the Low Church Bishop, Dr. Smoother was the High and Dry Bishop, Dr. Perkins was the Ritualistic Bishop, and Mr. Merler, who had the new Mission Church, was a sort of Bishop-at-large, and was at once, Low, High and Dry, and Ritualistic, as the necessity of his Episcopate demanded" (154). The only thing on which they agreed "was in the resisting any possible encroachment of the real Bishop" (155), who is cautioned by one of his episcopal brothers, the "prudent bishop of Laodicea," that "we Episcopal Bishops cannot expect to be anything more than machines for ordaining and confirming" (155). Because their main occupation is traveling, he proposes that their vestments should be a traveling overcoat, a "wide-awake" and a stout pair of boots; and their pastoral staff a railway pass on a sturdy cane. In fact, he goes on to say, since railway stations are becoming so attractive, it might be the most prudent use of time for Bishops to hold confirmation right there in the station, confirming two at a time.

So far the humor, though rueful, is good-natured, but as the advice proceeds, the tone becomes increasingly bitter: "'The Bishop, who tries to be a bishop, had better prepare himself for martyrdom; the stake they tie him to, will be his own Cathedral, they will pile Church newspapers around for faggots, all the rectors of the city, with their vestries, will stand about with Lucifer matches, and what a bonfire he will make'" (156).

Despite this advice, however, the Bishop of Dorchester persists in trying to be an authentic bishop, with what success is illustrated by the responses of each of the four other "bishops" to the notion that a Cathedral be established. Each speaks from his perspective, in comic reflection of the bias of each, and in doing so reveals that, in the effort to advance one's vested interest, there is no difference between a clergyman and any other person.

The conflict between the positions is made most explicit when two of the clergy and their wives find themselves on the same railway carriage as the Bishop and his wife, all on the same errand, to be with Robert Graham's grandmother as she approaches the end of her life. Mrs. Gooby has urged her husband, Zwingli, to attend Mrs. Graham for the opportunity it provides: "'Sometimes,' "she added, very solemnly," 'those High-Church people retract on their death beds, and get a justifying faith,'" (181). Mrs. Perkins (mother to three sons named Keble, Pusey and Newman, now called

Johnny), advises her husband George Herbert that it is his duty to attend Mrs. Graham's deathbed for a different reason: "'What if some Roman priest were to come along, and, with her views about confession, and all that, she was to go over to Rome, on her deathbed!'" (182). The Bishop and his wife are traveling to Mrs. Graham because she has written, imploring them to come, and because they love her.

While they are all six traveling together, the low churchman and the ritualistic clergyman fall into an argument about the relation of the Episcopal Church to the Roman Catholics on the one hand, and the Protestants on the other. This debate provides an opportunity for the Bishop of Dorchester to give voice to the "norm"—a key element in a satire. Part of a traditional satire includes not only poking fun at what is wrong, but also asserting what the author believes to be right.

As the Bishop addresses the Goobys and the Perkinses, we hear "'the Church did not stand midway, or any way, between Rome and Geneva; but moved on a different plane from both'" (184). He goes on to describe the flaws in the Episcopal Church in America, and his vision for its future in a stirring statement that voices Dr. DeKoven's own cherished beliefs: "'American Churchmen never yet believed in, much less practiced, their own Prayer Book.... The American Church,' cried the Bishop, 'is eagerly grasping after her own heritage, and God grant we may all advance until she gets it.... It will come, though; perhaps not in my day—the See, the Cathedral, the sisterhoods, the true ritual, the rightly ordered parishes, the solemn worship, the faithful laity. Then will the Church convert the land, and the belief in the Holy Catholic Church, in America, be a reality'" (185-6).

It is characteristic of Dr. DeKoven's narrative skill that this proclamation, though obviously heartfelt by speaker and author, is rescued from pomposity by humor. The driver, who has only partially heard the conversation, responds with a loud "Amen," thinking he has been listening to a Methodist prayer meeting.

The death of Mrs. Graham which these persons witness occurs simultaneously with the vindication of Robert, her grandson. This vindication occurs in large part because of Dr. Neverasole's involving himself with Robert's plight. Dr. Neverasole's involvement is so contrary to his previous behavior toward Robert that it seems he truly has been changed by the unusual series of encounters he has just experienced. This final focus on Dr. Neverasole is emphasized by a comment in the last chapter of the novel, and it provides an opportunity for one last denominational joke.

In this chapter the narrative voice distances itself from the story, becoming an oral story-teller, and the "reader" becomes the listener, who, like all readers, wants to know "what happens next?"

"'But what became of them all?' he persists. 'Did Dr. Neverasole become a Christian?'"

"'He became a Warden of the new Episcopal Church in Hubville, and was sent as a delegate to the Episcopal Convention,' I reply."

"'But did he become a Christian?'"

"'Of course, my dear; did you ever know a

delegate who was not one?'" (225).

So the story-teller concludes his tale with one of its strongest qualities: humor. Despite the moralizing of the novel which detracts from its appreciation by a modern reader, it has a strong appeal in its comic tone, especially when that comedy is self-directed. It is hard, however, to appreciate humor by reading only second-hand excerpts. The whole text should be read to get its full flavor. Of course, for that to be done conveniently would require the novel's being reprinted. But that, as the narrator of this story implies in his final comment to the little listener who persists in wanting to know "what happens next," would require another story altogether.

CHAPTER 4

A Brief History of Racine College

Jason Fout

The history of Racine College embraces humble beginnings, a glorious heyday, and a long struggle to survive. The school itself served at different times as a four-year college, junior college, military academy, and grammar school. Racine College claims as its own James DeKoven, "saintly, brilliant and outspoken," even recognized by the Episcopal Church in its Lesser Feasts, and yet the college struggled for support from the church. Although the school's history draws to a close after 81 years, the thousands of boys who studied at Racine College, many of whom eventually rose to prominence, bear witness to the life of a vital institution.

Beginnings (1850-1859)

In the early 1850s, the Rev. Dr. Joseph Nicols, rector of St. Luke's Episcopal Church in Racine, and the Rev. Dr. Azel Cole, president of Nashotah House seminary, approached the Episcopal Diocese of Wisconsin to propose founding an institution of higher learning. This would be a pioneering effort, since there was no other such school west of the Appalachian Mountains. The school would function as a preparatory school for Nashotah House, as well as a junior college.

Presenting their idea at the diocesan convention they found that several others, including Bishop Jackson Kemper, shared their vision. They held a contest between Racine and Milwaukee to see which could first raise $6,000 and six acres for the founding of the school. Racine won hands down, raising more than $10,000 from subscriptions and ten lakeside acres donated by Charles and Truman Wright.

The Board of Trustees of the newly named Racine College was incorporated March 3, 1852, and plans were made to open the school the following autumn with the Rev. Dr. Roswell Park as the college's first president. That May construction began on the campus's first building, named Park Hall for the incoming president.

In November of that year, Racine College began its session with nine students in a rented room, since Park Hall would not be finished until the following September. Dr. Park assumed all teaching responsibilities until three other professors joined him in 1853. The Rev. Joseph Nicols taught English literature, Marshall Strong taught political science, and General Philo H. Hoy taught the hard sciences. In addition, three younger assistants joined the staff that year. By the end of the first year the school enrolled 33 students and the future looked promising.

Dr. Park served in many capacities simultaneously during his seven-year tenure at Racine College, working as president, professor, chaplain, treasurer, fundraiser, overseer of new construction and curriculum developer—while also serving several years as rector St. Luke's parish!

A second building, Kemper Hall, had been constructed in 1857 at the south end of the Lake Michigan frontage and was identical to Park Hall. This new facility doubled the space of the college and allowed for 85 more students to attend. During these first seven years, the student body grew steadily, 43 students graduated, and the assets of the school expanded to almost $135,000.

The preparatory department of Racine College offered what we think of as high school instruction. The collegiate department offered two separate tracks, a four-year degree for students training for the "learned professions," and a two-year degree for boys preparing for "business pursuits." The former degree was called a Bachelor of Arts, and the latter a Bachelor of Science.

It is something of an open question whether or not Racine College was a church institution at this time. The founders, Doctors Cole and Nicols, said that "The interests of religion and political strengthening of the new West are so intimately interwoven with the morals of our settlers that secular education ought to be combined with Christian teaching," and furthermore that "The Church which has so actively participated in the opening of this frontier territory has an imperative duty to bring about that combination." Yet on the other hand the original charter does not mention it being a Church-affiliated school (despite the fact that the president and a majority of the Board were Episcopal clergy). The Board did modify the charter at the beginning of the second year so Racine College was officially an Episcopal college; nevertheless, boys of all denominations were admitted. Chapel was optional—and little attended.

Although Racine College had a somewhat ambiguous role as a church school, a number of students undertook preparatory work for Nashotah House. Additionally, many students and clergy associated with the college made significant contributions to the life of the Episcopal Church in Racine, working to develop over time several mission churches including Immanuel, St. Stephen's, Holy Innocents, St. Paul's, and St. Michael's.

Racine College under James DeKoven (1859-1879)

The year 1859 occasioned a financial crisis in America. While Racine College flourished with numerous graduates, impressive facilities, and growing assets, some feared what the national depression would bring. Seeking to guard against lean times, the college merged with St. John's Hall, a grammar school in Delafield, Wisconsin. Relocating to the campus of the college, St. John's brought with it a headmaster by the name of James DeKoven, who then became president of the combined institution. And so began the second phase of the college's life, by all accounts its heyday.

DeKoven brought his dedication and energy to Racine College, shaping its character directly for 20 years, and indirectly far beyond. He came to Wisconsin in 1854 from New York City, where he had studied at Columbia University and The General Theological Seminary, also doing outreach work with impoverished boys in lower Manhattan. Arriving in Wisconsin, he taught ecclesiastical history at Nashotah House, which was established only 12 years earlier. While continuing to teach at Nashotah, he became rector of St. John Chrysostom Episcopal Church in Delafield. DeKoven founded St. John's Hall, serving as its headmaster for five years. He saw the possibility of merger with Racine College to be providential. He sought to make the combined school more clearly a church college, as expressed in the new catalogue: "The object of this

Young grammar pupils

institution is to educate the youth placed in it through the agency of the Church, and in the principles of the Catholic Faith as held by the Protestant Episcopal Church in the United States and with an especial view, moreover, to the preparing for the study of theology, those intending to be clergymen."

DeKoven instituted a novel pattern for community life at Racine College in which faculty, their families, and the students lived together. Having observed this method in use in England (called the prefect system), DeKoven was the first to introduce it with success into an American school, and it was apparently popular with the students.

The year 1864 brought both loss and gain with it as Park Hall burned. The building suffered great damage as the library, classrooms, and chapel were completely destroyed. But in the wake of the destruction, sufficient funds were raised not only to rebuild

Park Hall but to construct a new chapel as well. St. John's Chapel, designed in the English Gothic style of the other buildings on campus, stands in the middle of the college grounds, communicating DeKoven's vision of the relationship between the college and the church. The chapel includes seating for three hundred, beautiful stained glass windows, a high altar, and a fine organ. The pews face each other across the aisle, collegiate style. DeKoven instituted daily choral services in the chapel, and began the first vested boys's choir west of the Appalachians. One of the architectural oddities is that several of the stained glass windows depict the saints as having six toes—doubtlessly a target for boyish humor during chapel services. The architecture

East End of St. John's Chapel

made possible another feature of chapel life: every May the sun would shine in from the west in the early evening and light brilliantly on the brass altar cross on a particular day. The boys often made bets on the date when this event would happen.

Racine College also purchased 80 more acres of land in 1864. It was used as farm land and provided the school with a source of food and income. The farm prospered along with the college, one year bearing over 1,000 bushels of potatoes, nearly 200 bushels of strawberries, as well as other produce.

In 1865, Isaac Taylor died. A friend of the college, he left an estate of $130,000 to be divided after his wife died between the college and a proposed orphanage. In 1867, Taylor Hall was constructed on the western edge of campus with the college's share of the estate. This new building provided sleeping quarters for fifty students, a library, five classrooms, and apartments for the warden and sub-warden (as the headmaster had come to be known). Eight years later, in February 1875, Taylor Hall burned due to a chimney fire. Funds were quickly raised to rebuild it and to construct a new gymnasium, both of which opened in 1876.

In the meantime, in 1871 and 1875, two other buildings were constructed between Park Hall and Kemper Hall, completing the eastern edge of the quadrangle. These buildings included a dining hall, classrooms, and an assembly hall.

The college's involvement in the surrounding community continued in the local mission churches, as well as with the Taylor Orphanage, St. Luke's Hospital, and a home for the aged.

Racine College Baseball Team

Racine College flourished under James DeKoven; enrollment climbed, the faculty increased in size and stature, and the school was largely self-supporting for some time. But the Episcopal Church, and the bishops in particular, offered the school little financial support. In June of 1876, DeKoven preached a stinging sermon haranguing the bishops to provide more support for the Episcopal college, the only one of its kind west of Kenyon College in Ohio. In response, the bishops of Colorado, Fond du Lac, Illinois, Indiana, Michigan, Missouri, Nebraska, Western Michigan and Wisconsin visited Racine College the following year and agreed to make it the official school of their dioceses. Unfortunately, talk exceeded action and very little came to fruition. The bishops generally did nothing once they returned to their dioceses.

Cadets from the Corps

James DeKoven died on March 19, 1879, at the age of 48. He was buried next to St. John's Chapel on the college grounds, where his shrine remains to this day.

Life after DeKoven (1879-1887)

The Rev. Dr. Stephen Parker succeeded DeKoven as president of the school and upheld much the same standards and customs established under DeKoven. Nevertheless, it seemed that much of the wind went out of Racine College's sails after DeKoven's death. Parker ably maintained the school, with enrollment hovering around 200, but very little growth was evidenced.

When Parker died in 1882, the Rev. Alexander Gray assumed the presidency of the college. At the church's General Convention in October, 1886, Gray led a pilgrimage of the deputies to DeKoven's grave. This journey was unprecedented and is particularly remarkable given the controversy and odium that surrounded DeKoven and his churchmanship during life. As an American apostle of the Oxford Movement, DeKoven was bitterly opposed by some unsympathetic churchmen. This amazing expedition of the convention seemed to be something of a conciliatory gesture in the shadow of his premature death.

Unfortunately, enrollment at Racine College dwindled under Gray's presidency until the collegiate department had to close in 1887.

Signs of Life; Decline and Closure (1887-1933)

The school opened the following autumn with the grammar school in operation, but with only

14 students, a fraction of the usual enrollment. Apparently it was not clear to people at first that only part of the school had closed, since they both operated under the name of Racine College. Enrollment continued to slip until the school convinced the Bishop of Chicago, the Rt. Rev. William McLaren, to assume administrative authority. He stepped in and reorganized the school in 1889, with the help of the Rev. Arthur Piper, rector of St. Luke's Church.

Piper had been a student at Racine under DeKoven, and had worked as a fellow, instructor and professor there while also serving at St. Luke's. Bishop McLaren appointed Piper president of the school, and he served as president for ten years until the work at St. Luke's demanded all his attention. That year, 1899, the Rev. Dr. Henry Robinson assumed presidency of the school. He had been headmaster under Piper and was himself a graduate of Racine College. Enrollment climbed under Piper and Robinson. In 1908, enrollment stood around 150, and Robinson departed to become Bishop of Nevada.

The Rev. Dr. William Shero followed Robinson as president and ably guided the institution for eight years. He raised the academic standards of the school. Shero left in 1916 to serve as rector of a church in Pennsylvania. Soon afterwards, the Rev. B. Talbot Rogers of Fond du Lac became president of the school.

At this time, universities and colleges asked preparatory schools to teach students for two additional years so that they could enter higher education at the beginning of their third (junior) year.

Such schools became known as "junior colleges," and Racine College again began to offer a two-year collegiate course. At the beginning of the 1916 school year, the enrollment stood at 95: 60 in the grammar school and 35 in the college.

In 1914 a commandant was added to the faculty and military drills were introduced for students, due in part to the gathering clouds of war over Europe. Four years later, the school changed its name to "Racine Academy," although most still knew it informally as Racine College.

Around this time enrollment declined. Other schools prospered and were able to offer their students more than Racine. Lean times ensued and the academy stumbled along until 1929, when the economic collapse caused the school to shut down completely.

In May of 1930, Racine Military Academy was organized and opened by several local men, including Lieutenant Colonel Earl Pearsall, Robert

Cushman, and Charles Stone. Junior and senior departments had facilities for 250 boys. In 1931, the University of Wisconsin recognized and accredited the school, and two years later it was reinstated as a junior college. Unfortunately, financial instability from the depression forced the school to close on August 8, 1933, concluding the history of the once-thriving Racine College, begun with such promise and support nearly 81 years earlier.

END NOTES

[1] Thomas C. Reeves, Essay in *Racine: Growth and Change in a Wisconsin County*, ed., by Nicholas C. Burckel, Racine, Wis.: Racine County Board of Supervisors, 1977.

[2] Sidney H. Croft, "A Hundred Years of Racine College and DeKoven Foundation." In *Wisconsin Magazine of History* (Summer 1952), 250.

[3] *Ibid.*, 251.

[4] *Ibid.*, 250.

[5] Croft, "A Hundred Years of Racine College and DeKoven Foundation," 251; Vicki K. Black, "A History of Racine College and The DeKoven Foundation." Unpublished essay, 2.

[6] Dorothy Osborne, "A History of Racine College" Unpublished essay, 4 "Celebrating an Era: St. Luke's Church 1842-1992." Unpublished history of St. Luke's Episcopal Church, Racine Wisconsin, author unattributed, 29.

[7] Black, "A History of Racine College and The DeKoven Foundation." Unpublished essay, 4; Sidney H. Croft, "Life of James DeKoven and Historical Sketch of Racine College." Unpublished thesis, on file at Nashotah House library (no page numbers).

[8] Black, "A History of Racine College and The DeKoven Foundation." Unpublished essay, 6.

[9] Croft, "A Hundred Years of Racine College and DeKoven Foundation," 253.

10 *Ibid.*, 253.

11 *Ibid.*, 254.

12 Sidney H. Croft, "Life of James DeKoven and Historical Sketch of Racine College." Unpublished thesis, on file at Nashotah House library (no page numbers).

13 Croft, "A Hundred Years of Racine College and DeKoven Foundation," 254.

14 *Ibid.*, 254.

CHAPTER 5

The DeKoven Foundation for Church Work:
The Middle Watch

Kitty Clark

Sometimes it happens. Seeds carefully planted in the garden come to bloom beside the fence. Events once set in motion move out in wide bands and then, unexpectedly, come back full circle. One American writer has suggested that life itself is like a minuet: people meet, their paths intersect, move into new patterns, and then come together again, as if part of some distant, far-off measure.

James DeKoven's influence on the national life of the Episcopal Church is well known. His influence on Racine College, the school he loved and, to a large extent, formed, is legendary. But there was another influence that must be mentioned here, because this influence is too much part of The DeKoven Center's history to pass over without notice.

The Community of Saint Mary was the first religious order for women in the Episcopal Church. It had a few supporters, yes—but one supporter was particularly vocal in the Community's behalf, offering friendship and encouragement when these were most needed. James DeKoven, whose own convictions were well known, and especially in General Convention, spoke always for the Episcopal Church's acceptance of its own full catholic heritage. He was an early champion of the religious life. His understanding and support proved to be the opening measure of the minuet.

Dr. DeKoven became president of Racine College in 1859, six years before the Community of St. Mary began settling into its life of ministry among the poor in New York. Outposts of the Community quickly spread: Sheltering Arms, a refuge for women and children; The House of Mercy, a refuge for prostitutes; St. Barnabas House, a similar work. Destitution was the only requirement to receive aid at any of these houses. Eight years after their founding in 1865, the Community opened the first children's hospital in New York City. The number of Sisters was increasing, support came from unexpected sources, here and there a champion emerged. James DeKoven knew the value of dedication like this, and the strength that grows in communal living. He spoke for the Sisters, wrote them his encouragement, gave them his blessing. The minuet pattern moved into place.

In 1877, Kemper Hall in Kenosha, Wisconsin, became available. Dr. DeKoven contacted the Sisters, urged them to come to Wisconsin and undertake the management of a school for young women, a work in education particularly dear to his own heart. Because of Dr. DeKoven's encouragement, the Sisters accepted Bishop Edward R. Welles's invitation and in 1878 took up their residency and their work at Kemper Hall. One year later, James DeKoven died, a tragic loss for this small group of Sisters who had come largely because of him.

But, in spite of it all, Kemper Hall flourished. The Community, not content with school work alone, quietly moved into the poorest neighborhoods of Chicago, establishing St. Mary's Home along with several other avenues of ministry. Racine College, unfortunately, never regained its full momentum after the death of James DeKoven.

In the summer of 1934, acting for the Board of Trustees, the Bishop of Milwaukee invited the Sisters to use the empty school buildings as a summer camp for girls from St. Mary's Home in Chicago. This was an important invitation for the Sisters. For several summers they had tried various places as a country setting for children whose lives were bounded by sidewalks and city streets. They accepted Bishop Ivins's invitation gladly.

Then in the fall of 1935, Racine College was put up for sale at a Sheriff's auction. The dream of James DeKoven, his prayer *Vigeat Radix*, "May the root thrive," had apparently come to an end. But the measure of the minuet had not ended.

Fifty-seven years after Dr. DeKoven's friendship had summoned the Community of St. Mary to Kenosha, these same Sisters rescued the historic property he loved so well. No other group of people, church or civic, stepped forward with enough money to save the College grounds. Without the Sisters, the buildings might have perished, the land perhaps given to commercial use, and the memory of Racine College would have faded with passing years.

The Sisters's purchase of the historic property was a remarkable rescue. But the purchase may also have happened because another pattern of the minuet was coming together. The earliest life of the Community of St. Mary had been among the poor of the cities. Now the same Sisters, in the name of the homeless children in Chicago, purchased the property from the Sheriff's block. Actual funds for the acquisition did not come from Kemper Hall, but from St. Mary's Home for Children.

So it was that the two sisters, Sr. Eanswith, the Sister in charge of St. Mary's Home for Children, and, "one other," moved into Taylor Hall and began the long process of renovating and reclaiming the east building. The first and most pressing task was to make this building habitable for their own summer camp, a safe and permanent place where children from tenements in Chicago would play in country sunlight.

With the purchase of Racine College, this dream was realized. Almost at once, the minuet passes into a new measure. Within two years the Sisters of St. Mary had incorporated the property under the title, The DeKoven Foundation for Church Work, the retreat ministry which continues today at The Dekoven Center.

They honored James DeKoven not only in naming the Foundation after him, but in commemorating his life by a special day each October. This day's celebration alone began to draw visitors to Racine from across the nation. By 1949 as many as 1,500 people were coming to The DeKoven Center each year for retreats and conferences. The Rt. Rev. Benjamin F. P. Ivins, the Bishop of Milwaukee, called DeKoven, "a treasure for the whole Church," and indeed it was. Today many dioceses have retreat centers, but in 1936 The DeKoven Center was unique.

At the time of the purchase, the East Building had already been occupied for two summers by St. Mary's Camp. A large dormitory room had been made habitable in the north end, the Park Building, with plenty of space all the way to the south end, the Kemper Building, for indoor camp activities. Meals were served in Racine College's Great Hall. The little girls from Chicago were enchanted. Even so, now that they owned the property, the Sisters could easily see exactly how much work remained to be done.

And then a new measure of the minuet began to move into place. Soon after its incorporation, The DeKoven Foundation separated its operation from the management of St. Mary's Home. By no means was the Camp work forgotten. For nearly 40 years the Camp retained its own life, under the direction of the Sisters with a staff of counselors to augment their work. But a new vision was emerging, and another calendar.

The selection of the name was "an obvious and happy choice," Sister Mary Bianca explained to the Priests' Institute in 1949. "We wanted to honor Dr.

DeKoven because of his intimate relationship with our community," she said.

Their clear goal was to establish a retreat and conference center in the spirit of James DeKoven's long vision for educational and spiritual formation, a goal that was to go far beyond their own expectations. "This is the Community's youngest work," Sister Mary Bianca told the clergy. "And like any youngster, it's growing faster than we can keep up with."

Eventually, the buildings themselves began to generate income. The south end of the East Building was made suitable to be leased to the Cove School, a school for children who were brain damaged at birth. The Gate House was remade into six apartments. Because of summer camp, St. Mary's Home again supplied funds for restoring the gymnasium and swimming pool.

St. John's Chapel was completely restored, organ and chimes reclaimed, and protective glass installed on all windows, making this historic building a place of worship, both for St. Mary's Camp in the summer, and for retreats and conferences during other months.

A gift from St. Luke's Church in 1938 enabled the Sisters to create a small chapel in Taylor Hall. This chapel, St. Mary's, with a carved wooden altar and furnishings, was perhaps another serendipity of the minuet. In his early years as President of Racine College, James DeKoven had helped lay the cornerstone for St. Luke's. From that time on, he maintained an affectionate and cordial relationship with the parish. The parish's gift of a chapel inside

Taylor Hall was gift indeed to this small band of Sisters whose rule required five hours a day of prayer.

Money for operating expenses and continuing upkeep of the buildings remained the Foundation's most pressing need in those early years. There was no resident domestic help and the Sisters worked ceaselessly, while maintaining their rigorous prayer schedule of Eucharist, prayer and offices.

In all of this, The DeKoven Foundation's goal was

clear and never failing. Sister Mary Bianca reminded the Priests' Institute, "It is fitting that here where James DeKoven labored for the cause of Christian education, an institution bearing his name should be carrying on a work that is so at one with his own aims and ideals."

In 1948 over 1,500 people attended conferences and retreats or came to The DeKoven Foundation as guests seeking, "Rest, quiet, study, prayer, or counsel." Five thousand received communion that year in the two chapels.

For a half-century, the Sisters maintained and operated The DeKoven Foundation for Church Work. Sister Mary Bianca followed Sister Eanswith, and in 1972 Sister Letitia became Sister-in-charge. The strong programs that had so quickly characterized the Sisters's work continued to attract nationally known leaders and bring hundreds of people to Racine from all over the country.

CHAPTER 6

The DeKoven Center, 1959 – 1986

Sister Dorcas Baker, C.S.M.

Father DeKoven's soul was set like a seal upon Racine College in the nineteenth century. The Sisters of St. Mary shaped the place throughout the twentieth century. Sister Eanswith and Sister Mary Valerie came to The DeKoven Center during the Great Depression, intrepidly repairing the ravaged buildings. Between 1934 and 1986, 25 Sisters of the Community of St. Mary worked at DeKoven. Sister Letitia and I were among those who were involved with both St. Mary's Camp and the retreat and conference ministry in the latter half of the twentieth century. That retreat ministry continues to flourish today, drawing creative depth from the vision the Sisters upheld.

The DeKoven Sisters worked very hard in the first 25 years to restore the old buildings and build up a viable retreat ministry. They were totally dependent on the generous support of associates, friends, and the Episcopal Church Women (ECW) plus income from a small trust which was set up for Racine College and transferred to the Sisters.

Taylor Hall had a dirt floor basement, only one bathroom in the whole building, no elevator nor dumb waiter, large rooms which had to be divided to provide more bedrooms for guests, no fire escapes, no fire doors, no chapel, no car.

Sister Mary Valerie used to collect trading stamps to purchase various items needed. The Fifth Province ECW sponsored a campaign to donate trading stamps so the Sisters could buy a car. It took seven months to accumulate enough for the purpose. The "Stamp Wagon" became the first car at DeKoven.

When Sister Mary Bianca was appointed Superior of DeKoven in 1958, she insisted that the full Divine Office (Benedictine style) be said (or sung when possible) just as it was at the convent in Kenosha. It was said along with all the extra seasonal devotions such as the Stations of the Cross and the whole drama of Holy Week. But she was also open to the winds of liturgical reform which began to blow in the 1960s. Prayer Book Offices replaced the Divine Office making it much easier for guests to participate in worship with the Sisters. We experimented with various trial liturgies which preceded the present Prayer Book, and began standing for the Eucharistic Prayer.

The community was also undergoing changes. Most noticeably, the religious habit began to change in the mid-1960s. Soft linen replaced the starched wings. The skirts were shortened and black (or blue) dresses replaced the formal habit. By 1969 the habit had vanished altogether, except for some of the older

**Taylor Hall Retreat and Conference Center,
The DeKoven Center**

Sisters who still wished to wear it. For a few years most of the Sisters kept a simple black veil to wear for formal occasions, but eventually even that disappeared. It was good to look and be treated like an ordinary human being. Habits do not make their wearers any better or holier than they are without them, but people love to project their own potential holiness onto clergy and religious. It was also good to wear clothing that was comfortable, easy to work in, and easy to wash. Nevertheless, some of us missed the freedom of not having to maintain even a small wardrobe. For those who came to the community very young, before developing a strong sense of personal identity, the habit could be an attractive cover at an unconscious level, a hiding place providing a false sense of identity and belonging.

In 1969 Sister Mary Bianca retired and for three years the Sisters at DeKoven experimented with having no single Sister-in-Charge. We made all decisions as a group. It worked well for us, but outsiders found it difficult not to have a person with whom to deal. So in 1972 we decided Sister Letitia should be formally blessed as Sister-in-Charge. She had already taken charge of St. Mary's Camp in 1969.

Letitia, Jean and I were the only Sisters permanently on the staff after 1969. Mary Valerie continued with us until she retired to the Convent in 1976. Lucia, Mary Martha, and Mary Dunstan helped with the Camp for several summers. Jane Francis lived with us in Taylor Hall while she studied nursing. Mary Martha was with us full time for a couple of years before volunteering as a medical missionary in Nicaragua. The early 1970s were a time of great change for the community. The Convent Sisters were working on revising the Rule. Sisters working in branch houses like DeKoven often felt a bit like second class citizens in the community. The DeKoven Sisters left the Rule revision to the

Convent and concentrated on revisions of their own that were more related to lifestyle than the Rule. Mary Martha's mother was a champion of ecology long before that became a popular concern. While Mary Martha was on the staff, she inspired us to embrace this issue.

The first step we took was to flatten tin cans and save glass jars for recycling. Actually, Jean had been recycling paper, boxes and packing materials for her bookstore and mail order business for years just to save money.

The rising cost of food, abundance of space, shifting summer job schedules, and a sheer spirit of adventure led us to try a vegetable garden. I planted it in some dozen five inch by thirty-five inch strips with equal grass space between each. Although this method had some drawbacks in terms of machine tilling and required eternal vigilance against encroachment of grass, one rarely had to set foot in the growing area which made a minimum tillage method of spadework quite adequate. It was also a very convenient and attractive layout, and compost and fertilizer could be concentrated on the growing area.

At about the same time the garden was launched, we became concerned about what to do with 32 acres of oak and maple leaves. Burning was no longer permitted in the city. First we tried dumping them in a designated compost pile. But the leaves would not stay put, even with a snow fence around them. Finally we had to dump a load of dirt on them to anchor the pile. Then we dug a series of four compost pits in ten foot squares to be used in a four year cycle: filled one year, left for three and then emptied onto the garden. This method accommodated some leaves, most of the grass clippings, and nearly all of the kitchen garbage, not to mention the weeds in the garden. The garbage disposal unit became obsolete except when the snow was too deep to get to the compost pit.

During the summer of 1976 we decided to stop mowing about a third of the grounds for several reasons. We were concerned that many of the ancient oaks were being felled by storms and it was impossible to continue replanting the trees by hand. Also, we came to understand that the red oaks on the property represented almost the only original stand of oaks in the Racine area, and we wanted to give them a chance to re-seed themselves. We were also interested in allowing native wild flowers to grow, and in letting the fallen leaves go back into the soil. The neighbors, however, did not share our vision. There was a siege of complaints about the grounds. With the help of Lorrie Otto, a champion of natural landscaping in Milwaukee, we persuaded the city authorities to allow us not to mow. Gradually the neighbors got used to the new look and the complaints died away. Pheasants returned after many years of exile.

Another external pressure toward change was brought to bear on the DeKoven Sisters by the rising cost of natural gas in the mid 1970s. After Mary Valerie retired, the bookkeeping fell to me, and the budget became a group concern. My father had been a CPA and I vowed I would never do any kind of accounting. Life has an inscrutable way of making us eat our words.

A three-sided war began against the heating bills: the roofs were insulated, storm windows and doors were purchased and the thermostat was turned down. The temperature inside was 62 to 65 during the day and 55 at night. The Sisters bought plenty of long underwear, heavy socks and sweaters, and made good use of the two operable fireplaces on the first floor with wood from the fallen oaks. Julia Peyton was then living in the East Building and acting as manager for the various tenants. She had previously been working for the Sisters as housekeeper in Taylor Hall for several years. Her job was to get as much of the building occupied as possible. Tenants included the Racine Montessori School (which actually began in the basement of Taylor Hall during Sister Mary Bianca's time), a Day Care Center, a number of artist studios, the Racine County Housing Authority headquarters (who helped the Sisters get federal funds for maintaining and renovating the buildings, since they had been listed on the National Register), the Spectrum School of Art, and several apartments.

About this time DeKoven received a very generous gift from Mrs. Harriet Cleaver. This was invested. For the first time DeKoven had an endowment fund producing interest to supplement the operating income. That fund had grown to nearly half a million dollars by the time the Sisters left DeKoven.

In the spring of 1974 the Sisters read aloud together Agnes Sanford's autobiography, *Sealed Orders*. This inspired us to begin a corporate experiment in prayer and fasting on a regular basis. We began with one day every fortnight fasting until dinner and keeping a constant prayer vigil in chapel from after Morning Prayer until dinner. Each Sister took two one-hour shifts. We agreed beforehand on a particular intention for the day, often for healing for people who had asked our prayers, but also for guidance and growth toward wholeness for ourselves and our Community. At first we thought of fasting only as an aid to intercession, but it soon occurred to us that we could make our fasting an offering to the hungry by sending the money saved from the meals we skipped to the Presiding Bishop's Fund for World Relief. One Lent we decided to step up the prayer/fast days to one day every week. We continued at that pace for the rest of our time at DeKoven.

While all this was going on at DeKoven, the Sisters at the Convent in Kenosha withdrew from managing Kemper Hall, the boarding school which the Community had run since 1878, and moved to Milwaukee. That was in 1974, the very year we read *Sealed Orders* and began our prayer/fast days. Sister Vlasta Mari was the Mother Superior at the time and she had put a tremendous amount of time and energy into the whole relocation project. We chose to pray for her on our first prayer/fast day. She died of a heart attack within a week. That shook us up badly, but as we pondered and prayed, it seemed to us that she had accomplished the task she had set about to do. The burden of leadership is a heavy one, and we thought she must have been glad to lay it down.

Over the next couple of years all of us at DeKoven

attended one or more of the Schools of Pastoral Care which Agnes Sanford founded to teach clergy about healing prayer. We hosted several of these schools at DeKoven. To one of these I brought a badly broken relationship as well as a prayer that I would be given a key to my own personal healing, and growth in maturity. When I got home, I wrote the estranged woman a reconciling letter, but just as it was with the prodigal son, I received the love before my letter reached her. Her letter of apology crossed mine in the mail. Some days later I wrote my mother about the School, telling her how I had broken down and wept at the closing consecration service. My mother replied that she was amazed because she could not remember me ever crying as a child. I understood that the key which had been given to me was simply the permission to be human, to make mistakes, to forgive and be forgiven.

The experiments with gardening and conservation took on a new spiritual dimension after reading *The Findhorn Garden*. We had been thinking in purely pragmatic terms of economics and ecology. It had become clear that the garden was probably costing us more in terms of labor than the value of the (still undeniably fresher and more delicious) vegetables our garden was producing. *The Findhorn Garden* helped us see that the battle against pollution and for better stewardship of creation was too small a goal. Beyond these lay the call to live in harmony with the earth, as well as with one another. The Lord put Adam in the garden not just to eat from it, but to "till it and keep it." So all our striving for social justice and against hunger, poverty and disease must also be a striving for loving partnership with our elemental partners, instead of cold and calculating usury. In light of these insights, the garden became more than just a way to cut the food bill. It became a school for learning how to work with earth and sun and water and a host of living, growing things.

We took a new look at the kinds of food we were eating because of the example of the Findhorn people, who ate almost nothing but the things they had grown themselves. We were also influenced by information we received from Bread for the World. We decided we could do with much less meat, (not so much because it was expensive in terms of money, but because of its cost in terms of the grain required to produce it), and much simpler, healthier desserts like fruit. We began avoiding ready-made, instant foods and the whole battery of artificial flavors and preservatives. After we sold the soft drink machine, we began providing fruit and tomato juice for our guests. We also joined a food co-op and began buying eggs, cheese, various grains, and legumes there. The gift of a table model hand-powered flour mill inspired us to begin making our own whole wheat bread and altar bread.

One more book gave the Sisters the final push into the vegetarian world: *Cooking with Conscience*. The recipes in this little cookbook were arranged in some 40 menus, each of which was worked out to contain a complete protein substitute for meat. It also explained how to plan meatless meals that provide all the protein required for good nutrition. The ready-made menus made it easy to begin. With this book as guide, we plunged into an almost totally meatless and sweetless Lent (1978). Since we felt we had a unique opportunity to share our dietary (and liturgical) experiments with the people who came to DeKoven for retreats and conferences, we began to inflict *Cooking with Conscience* menus on our guests. We also provided written explanation of what we were trying to do and why—but not without some trepidation. Our fears, however, proved groundless. With the exception of a couple of laments over the absence of rare roast beef or a good old hamburger, the overall result was the sale of some 175 copies of *Cooking with Conscience* in our bookstore over a six month period.

When the city of Racine began to charge residents for sewerage treatment along with the water bill instead of using tax money, the DeKoven water bill doubled overnight. Since DeKoven was tax exempt, this meant that we were paying for sewerage treatment for the first time, which was perfectly reasonable. Water was no longer taken for granted, and efforts to reduce our water consumption took the form of new shower heads for all the buildings with buttons on them so they could be turned off easily while soaping. We also became more careful about running water unnecessarily—for example, when brushing teeth. In order to use less paper, we stopped using paper place mats in the dining room and replaced paper napkins with cloth.

Another thread of our lives during our last 20 years at DeKoven was dance. It had its inception at St. Mary's camp in the late 1960s. Some of the counselors we hired to staff the Camp had learned folk dance at college. It struck us as a wonderful activity to offer the campers. Neither Letitia nor I had ever danced before. However, my mother had been a professional ballet dancer for many years. My dance experience was limited to deadly social dance classes in junior high school, then six weeks of ballet one summer after high school graduation. So we bought a set of six LP records with a book of instructions for over a hundred folk dances from all over the western world. We taught ourselves the dances and then taught the children. I think we enjoyed the dances as much as or more than the children.

An Israeli dance called Mayim was one of the dances we taught. The words of many Israeli dances come from Scripture, particularly the Psalms. Mayim is a dance of religious thanksgiving for having found water in the desert. Camp ran for six weeks, divided into three two-week sessions. We had an outdoor Eucharist once each session. The children who had learned Mayim danced it at the offertory of the outdoor Eucharists. It was the beginning of what we have come to call Sacred Congregational Dance.

Meanwhile, many of the younger Sisters in the community were going back to school for various kinds of professional training: nursing, social work, communications. Thinking that non-institutional work might be the direction of the future, I began training in music therapy. I never completed the course, but at the University of Wisconsin-Parkside I noticed a flyer on the bulletin board one day about an International Folk Dance group which danced on Friday evenings in Racine. Letitia and I decided to try it, and fell in love with both the dances and the people. That was another turning point in our journey. It was not long before we were leading a small group of the dancers who wanted to dance more than once a week and concentrate on the most challenging dances. We even made ourselves costumes and performed occasionally for schools, nursing homes and other places.

When Sr. Mary Valerie retired, we had to give up dancing on Friday evenings since most of our retreats and conferences began on Fridays. We needed to be home to register our guests and get them settled. But we continued to lead the dance group at DeKoven.

From the International Dancers we learned about Summer Dance Camps. In 1976 we attended the Kentucky Dance Institute, a one-week dance camp. It was the first time we ever had a vacation that was not visiting family, or another house of the Community. We had a great time and were named the flying nuns after dancing a two-couple dance with two strong men who lifted both of us off our feet in a fast spinning circle. It was at that camp that we met Russ Acton, a gentleman farmer and devoted patron of folk dance. He gave us a rebuilt phonograph with variable speed (16 rpm to 78 rpm and all grades in between). It had enough volume to fill the DeKoven gym.

The gym, which was used by the Camp during the summer, was rented by many local basketball and volleyball teams during the winter. The pool was used for swimming lessons and pool parties. Jean managed the scheduling, opening and locking up, and receipt of custom for the gym and pool through most of the 1970s, in addition to running a first-rate bookstore with the help of a good bookkeeper. She was great at finding and stocking the store with wonderful books and also a most welcoming hostess to all our guests.

By the 1970s the gym floor was badly in need of repair. Johnson Wax Company offered a matching grant to replace it, and the Dioceses of Milwaukee and Chicago rose to the occasion with half the money needed. The new floor was a sprung parquet wood floor which was both gorgeous to behold and welcomed by the folk dancers. It had so much bounce that we had to put the record player on the terrazzo vestibule to keep the records from jumping.

At the Kentucky Dance Institute we learned a Scottish Country dance called the Robertson Rant. We bought the record and brought the dance home to our own group because we loved the music so much. Little did we know that within six years our group would no longer be an international dance group but wholly Scottish Country. For the next several summers, Letitia and I attended Maine Folk Dance Camp run by the very people who were responsible for the book and records which were our first teachers. One of the classes each day was all Scottish Country. We were hooked. From the teacher we learned that there was a Summer School for Scottish Country Dance in Canada, and we attended it for the first time in 1982. For the next four years we progressed through the graded classes for Scottish Country Dance, and in 1986 I passed the Preliminary Teacher Certificate exam. (I had been teaching since the late 1960s, but the Royal Scottish

Country Dance Society in Edinburgh endeavors to maintain a uniform and high standard of teaching to preserve the authentic Scottish style and spirit.)

It was also in 1986 that the Sisters turned the management of The DeKoven Center over to the Diocese of Milwaukee. Jean elected to move into the East Building where Mary Grace was already living after the sale of the Convent in Milwaukee in 1984. Letitia and I were allowed to create an apartment in Taylor Hall out of the rooms that we had always occupied. Our efforts to find another location had not been fruitful, but it was like living in the house you built and cherished while watching the new owners remodel it. In the community it is wise for a retiring Superior to take a sabbatical or move to a different house when her successor takes the reigns. In 1987, Letitia and I put our furniture in storage at St. Luke's Church and went to Rome for a year of study, travel, and spiritual renewal.

At first our interest in dance was purely recreational, but as we experienced the power of dance to unite people of different ages, nationalities, classes, backgrounds, creeds, and colors, we began to ponder how to bring this experience into our worship. It was not long before we discovered how easily many of the steps and patterns of folk dances (especially Israeli ones) could be used to choreograph hymns. The first one to be choreographed was, not surprisingly, "Lord of the Dance." Diarmuid O'Murchu writes in his book, *Quantum Theology*, that "Dance is the first, most ancient and most enduring form of religion." Since the dawn of human history, dance has been used as a means of expressing

St. Mary's Chapel during Eastertide,
Taylor Hall, The DeKoven Center

religious feeling. Dance and song require only the human body to perform and are thus the logical first instruments of worship.

It was the simple, inclusive circle dances that we wanted to introduce into church. But architecture barred the way. The circle had already become our way of decision making. Now we wanted our worship to be circular in form as well. After our week at Maine Camp one summer, we spent a few days at Madonna House in Ontario, the Community which Catherine Dougherty founded. We had read her book *Poustinia,* and wanted to try a day in one of her hermitages. We were not impressed with the community, and the hermitage was not heaven. But the chapel they had built (out of the wood and stone of the land) was breathtakingly beautiful. It was built to accommodate both Eastern and Roman

Rites. The congregational space was square with four pillars supporting the central dome. There were no pews or seats of any kind except for a built-in bench running around the outside wall for those who could not sit on the floor or stand for a long time. The floor was highly polished unstained wood. Books were kept on shelves in the entry way. When we got home, we took the pews out of St. Mary's Chapel in Taylor Hall, and had the Studios of Potente build a free standing altar. We had the floor sanded and refinished without staining. At first we put in benches from the East Dining Hall, but found that chairs were better for sore backs and easier to arrange. For ourselves, we kept a semicircle of benches around the altar which we put in the middle of what had been the Sisters's choir (except when we needed maximum seating capacity in the chapel). Our maintenance man built wooden boxes for the center of each bench in which we could keep our prayer books and hymnals. Each box had an oil lamp on it so we could say Compline by lamp light. Meanwhile, Father Travis Du Priest, one of our priest friends who celebrated the Eucharist for us once a week, had discovered and built for himself a meditation bench. He showed it to us and we begged him to make one for each of us. Bare floors are not the kindest foundation for such benches, so we cut some carpeting into kneeling pads.

Now dancing around the altar was possible. We began dancing hymns for special occasions. Then we introduced our dances to some of the retreat groups we sponsored. These people went home and told their friends. We began to receive requests to come to parishes and present dance workshops on Saturdays in preparation for the Sunday Eucharist. Although we loved doing this, it was frustrating because we were usually limited to aisle space. This meant the dances had to be processional or recessional in form. Moreover, the number of dancers was usually between eight and 20, so it was impossible to escape the audience-performance mentality.

Our vision for dance in worship is that it should include everyone in the congregation who is able to walk. Its purpose is to provide us with an *image* and an *experience* of being connected, with the equality and interdependence in which we are meant to live as members of the Body of Christ, and citizens of One World. This is an image and an experience to give us a vision for the renewal of corporate worship, and the healing of our strife-torn world.

Meanwhile, in 1977, the Community was going through much turmoil. Sister Mary Joan had succeeded Sister Vlasta Mari as Superior at the Convent. Shortly thereafter a very promising young Novice died of asthma in her arms on the way to the hospital. Mary Joan had been elected a delegate to the General Convention which voted to admit women to the priesthood. There was dissension in the community over the issue, and many Associates resigned or transferred to the Eastern Province because Mary Joan had supported the ordination of women. Sometime in the spring of 1977, Mary Joan, Mary Martha, and the last remaining Novice left the Community. It was a heavy blow from which the Western Province of the Community of St. Mary may never recover.

I was now the youngest member of the Community and the only one left of my generation. There were too few Sisters left to staff both the Camp and the Retreat Ministry. The Camp which had operated for over 40 summers had to be closed. Two years later the pool was also closed; the building was in need of major repairs. We repaired the pool, and then just let it stand unused.

At DeKoven, while our vision for the future continued to grow and glow with promise, the cost of maintaining the place kept rising and we knew that everything must be used to capacity if it were to remain financially viable. To this end, we hired the Carley Capital Group in 1980 to do a market survey regarding possible new uses for the property. They led us to believe they were interested in the innovative ideas and ecological concerns we valued, such as turning the swimming pool into a fish hatchery, and building bio-shelters on the north campus which would require no outside sources of energy to operate. These would be teaching examples of earth friendly habitation. Also planned was the building of a methane heating plant by tapping into the city sewerage, which is treated in a plant next door to DeKoven. At the end of the two year study, the only suggestion Carley Capital produced was one for rather expensive housing on the north campus. Their one concession to our ecological concerns was to berm the north sides of the buildings with about four feet of dirt.

Meanwhile, in 1980, DeKoven became the locus of the Novitiate for the community. By this time there were only three Sisters left on the DeKoven staff. Four women tried their vocations with us during the next six years, but none stayed. I think we tried too hard to accommodate our life to suit the Novices. The retreat and conference work suffered. We were forced to cut back the schedule in order to make time to try to build community with the new people. But we had no model for training Novices except the one we had lived more than a generation earlier, and we were not good at expressing our expectations. There were some wonderful times during those years, but it was also a difficult and stressful period. And it was the final sign that led us to the decision to leave DeKoven while it was still viable and operating in the black financially, and while we still had enough energy to start over with something new.

Jean is now living at St. John's Home in Milwaukee. Three other Sisters are living in St. John's Tower Apartments, also in Milwaukee. Letitia was elected Superior of the community in 1992. For five years after our sabbatical year in Rome, Letitia and I lived in a rented house in Mukwonago. Friends and Associates followed us there, and we found ourselves back in a ministry of hospitality, but now small, intimate and enjoyable. (One of the best parts of our years at DeKoven was the ministry to individual guests who were usually housed in the "Convent Hilton." These guests shared the background life of the Sisters and became special friends.)

When Father Du Priest became the director of The DeKoven Center in 1991, Letitia and I drove down one day a week to help with the bookkeeping. By this time it became clear that we should buy a house of our own to accommodate guests. In 1993,

One of many social gatherings and receptions in the Great Hall at The DeKoven Center

we bought a house only a mile or so from where we had been living. It is Mary's Margin, and here we continue our ministry of hospitality to individuals and small day groups. We founded a new Scottish Country Dance group in Milwaukee which is now officially affiliated with the Royal Scottish Country Dance Society. I passed the full Teacher Certification Exam and hold the official Teacher's Certificate. Father Du Priest is our chaplain for Saturday or Sunday Eucharists and community meetings.

Already the ministry has grown beyond our capacity. The solution has been the creation of a program which we call the "Nun/Monk Corps," a kind of Inner Peace Corps. It is for students or people in transition who want to take a year or two of time out, share our life, and work for room and board to assist with the ministry. Now in its third year of operation, the Corps has been an immense blessing for us and the participants.

CHAPTER 7

DeKoven: Holy Man, Holy Place

"In every life God raises up holy places where he means us to find him."

(Quotation by Archbishop of Canterbury Robert Runcie in the Runcie Common Room of Taylor Hall)

Travis Talmadge Du Priest

I don't always get "the last word," so in this case I am pleased to be offered it. First, because it allows me the opportunity to pay homage to "the cloud of witnesses" in the past who made Racine College and The DeKoven Foundation the lively, viable institutions they were and are today: Dr. Rosewell Park, the first president of the college; "Blessed James DeKoven," our patron saint; the numerous members of the Community of St. Mary who rescued this precious property and had the foresight to found St. Mary's Camp for Girls and The DeKoven Foundation for Church Work in the 1930s; the countless members of the local Racine community who fought so hard to save the historic property from development in the 1990s; and to our patrons and

Fr. Du Priest, director, at The DeKoven Center with the community of St. Mary Sisters (Western Province) on the occasion of his 25th anniversary of ordination.

benefactors who made the repurchase and initial renovations on the property by The DeKoven Foundation possible.

Second, because it allows me the opportunity to thank the scores of people who have made this book possible, especially the researchers and contributors to the various chapters, the photographers and technical support people, and, of course, Dr. Rob Slocum, who has overseen the shape of the project.

And third, because it allows me to assure readers of this book and visitors to this historic place that The DeKoven Foundation is alive and well—indeed, flourishing—today.

Whenever I have the opportunity to welcome groups or tourists to the Center, I like to use the phrasing: "Welcome to The DeKoven Center, a place of education, recreation, and spiritual reflection for

150 years." True, we are no longer Racine College, though we live and work on its campus; true, the Community of St. Mary no longer operates the Center, though our board, an historical entity of the Episcopal Diocese of Milwaukee but today made up of over half local Racine citizens, continues in an unbroken line the retreat and conference ministry of The DeKoven Foundation for Church Work begun by the Sisters in the late 1930s.

In an interesting and almost miraculous way, the actual work that goes on today at The DeKoven Center has been for all intents and purposes unbroken since 1852. Yes, the campus and historic quadrangle have housed the prestigious Racine College, Racine Military Academy which educated some of our nation's best known leaders, the Center of Devotion and Conference for the national Episcopal Church, The DeKoven Foundation for Church Work, the Oriental Students Conference (of the University of Chicago, now Brent House), the Cove School for mentally challenged children, St. Mary's Camp for Girls which ran until 1977, two Religious Communities—the Community of St. Mary (C.S.M.) and in the late 1980s for several years, the Order of Julian of Norwich (O.J.N.), numerous artists's studios, and for some 25 years Racine Montesorri School.

There have also been times of incredible challenge and struggle—at the turn of the century when new visions were needed for the campus to continue as a place of education; in the early 1930s as the Depression necessitated the closing of the school here; and in the mid-1990s as the diocese lost the property due to a default on the Lake Oaks housing project for seniors. Lake Oaks was a painfully ironic situation because the project was conceived to ensure the stability of DeKoven's future. After Lake Oaks defaulted on the housing property, the entire historic property went into receivership and then under the ownership and oversight of a property development firm in Madison, Wisconsin. In each case, the future was threatening for this precious land and its historic buildings. But in each case, friends in the community emerged to fight the good fight and continue the DeKoven tradition.

In the 1920s the Cushman family of Racine fought to keep the school open, and Bishop Ivins and the Community of St. Mary acquired the property for St. Mary's Camp for Girls and subsequently The DeKoven Foundation. And in the mid-1990s, thousands of local Racine citizens participated in efforts for several years to regain local ownership and operation of the property. This included town meetings, the signing of petitions, and the arduous commitment of The DeKoven Community Center.

Substantial funds were raised by the Community of St. Mary, the Kingston Ehrlich family, Gene Miller, John Hart, Josephine McNeil-Lewis, and countless other Racine citizens, and with a matching grant of $300,000 from S. C. Johnson, Inc., The DeKoven Foundation was able to repurchase the property and begin important restoration work. Since the repurchase of the historic property in 1998, we have received grants totaling well over a million dollars and much needed restoration has been done on the inside and outside of Taylor Hall, St. John's

Chapel, and the East Building. Outside walkways have been restored, new exterior lighting installed, and handicap accessible entrances built. The major renovation of the Gym and Pool was extended and paid off. This work was largely completed in 1991 to the thrill of the whole community.

Also numerous smaller grants have enabled us to plan day camps for local children, provided nationally-known speakers and leaders for our conferences and retreats, and embark on wide-scale local cooperative programming for the local and regional community. The Center today offers more sponsored conferences, seminars, programs—educational, spiritual and recreational—than ever before. And the unique atmosphere of quietude and serenity lingers.

That several religious communities have lived here attests to DeKoven's atmosphere of spirituality: a place, like Little Gidding for T. S. Eliot, where prayer has been valid. In addition to running The DeKoven Foundation, DeKoven became the place where women tried their vocations for the Community of St. Mary. Since 1975 (when I first met the Sisters), a number of women—young and middle aged—have lived in community with the Sisters while considering the religious life. And in recent years, since 1985 when the Foundation and the historic property were transferred to the Episcopal Diocese of Milwaukee, at least ten young men and women have come to and through DeKoven on their way toward religious communities. The place seems to provide that liminal space necessary for godly discernment. Three men have gone on to take vows, and a fourth will soon do so; and two women have joined communities. Several are still exploring the religious life and regularly stay in touch with DeKoven.

These men and women are, of course, over and above the hundreds of retreatants who pass through DeKoven each year, many of whom count DeKoven as "their spiritual home," returning year after year to renew their spirits and be surrounded by the sense of the numinous that resides on campus and throughout the historic chapels and hallways. DeKoven might be properly termed "a secular religious house," no longer the home of a specific religious community, but home to a "community of communities." DeKoven has the hallowed aura of a shrine or special holy place.

One of the great gifts in the 1990s was the raising up of a religious solitary, Sister Brigit-Carol, S.D. (Solitary of DeKoven), believed to be the first professed religious of the Episcopal Church to take Blessed James DeKoven as her patron saint. Another gift: The Community of St.Mary has allowed its annual Associates's Retreat to evolve into a Friends of DeKoven retreat.

In all the various institutional embodiments, DeKoven's focus has continued to be on education, recreation, and spiritual reflection. Today, The DeKoven Center is home to The DeKoven Foundation for Church Work, which sponsors monthly retreats, quiet days, conferences, and special events designed to call men and women to deeper awareness of the still center of their lives. The Foundation has been blessed in recent years with two small but growing endowments to undergird its work: The

Summer retreatants in Taylor Hall Dining Room, The DeKoven Center

Katherine Greer Clark Retreat Scholarship Fund and the Alice Lowry Chapel Fund. The Epiphany Foundation of Cincinnati, Ohio, has underwritten several special retreats and made it possible for DeKoven to invite nationally and internationally known retreat leaders and writers.

The DeKoven Center also sponsors a full-scale recreation program for the community. Its gymnasium and swimming pool serve as an adjunct to our retreat and conference work. In fact, during our Meditation Intensive Retreat each summer, we encourage those who wish to try a floating meditation in the pool. Our Wedding Coordinator oversees weddings, concerts, and services which take place in historic St. John's Chapel and The Great Hall.

We have also sponsored and hosted up to four youth day camps per summer on our campus, including Kindercamp for physically challenged children and our own Sustainable Arts Day Camp, and art camps sponsored by Spectrum School for the Arts.

Over and above these sponsored events through the auspices of The DeKoven Foundation, DeKoven Center hosts a number of other not-for-profit institutions compatible with its mission and community service: Spectrum School for the Arts; Crossroads, a national anti-racism organization; Kindermusic School for Children; New Covenant Church; and Original Root Meditation Center. We also welcome individuals and groups to use our facilities, all of which are open to the public for meetings, conferences, retreats, parties, social and cultural events, and public service benefits.

While The DeKoven Center has increasingly opened its doors to its neighbors and the community through programming and facility usage, it has never lost its national scope and continues to attract nationally and internationally known speakers and writers to campus. In recent years, we have hosted authors Madeleine L'Engle, Stephanie Cowell, Gail Godwin, Suzanne Guthrie, and Ann Weems; retreat conductors such as Alan Jones and Margaret Guenther; and a spectrum of clergy such as Archbishop of Canterbury, Lord Robert Runcie, Presiding Bishop Frank Griswold, former Bishop of Chicago James Montgomery, as well as religious from numerous orders within the church.

Along with the well known personalities who visited the old college such as Mary Todd Lincoln and Ralph Waldo Emerson, and locals who attended such as General "Billy" Mitchell, Kingston ("King") Ehrlich, and F. H. Johnson, DeKoven has continued to attract its share of luminaries.

Yet it is for the unnamed and unknown that we largely exist—those who seek us out as "a place apart" for rest, refreshment, and reinvigoration of body, mind, and spirit. The countless retreatants, conferees, and patrons in the gym and pool, brides and grooms in the chapel, children at schools and camps on campus, and local friends who visit us for weekly Chapel or for Christmas at DeKoven. For these who come and go, for those who sometimes stay for awhile—it is for these friends that we are here.

Over the years, I have come to see my role as director of DeKoven not so much as an executive but rather as an innkeeper. DeKoven's primary ministry is to welcome—to welcome the lonely, the hurt, the seeker, as well as to provide hospitality to the joyous, the happy, those who have reason to celebrate. Some arrive in need of rest and reflection; others arrive full of energy, hoping to evolve and contribute to the stability and beauty of the campus. Some arrive full of faith; others arrive full of doubts. Some arrive alone, some in large groups. Our work is to welcome each and every one and to provide safety, peace, and understanding; and when possible, nourishment for body, mind, and spirit.

One priest recounts receiving his call to the priesthood on retreat in St. Mary's Chapel in Taylor Hall; a former "Camp Girl" visiting from California points to the prie dieu she made years ago at Kemper

Carved wood Mary and Christ Child in St. Mary's Chapel, Taylor Hall, The DeKoven Center

Hall. A laywoman from the Diocese of West Texas has modeled their diocesan retreat on the annual "Long Retreat" held for Friends of DeKoven and CSM Associates, and returns each summer with her dog and air-conditioned camper. Whether it be a carved wooden cross on a newel post, a Gothic insert in a lancet window, a hanging plant in the dining room, the beautiful carved reredos in St. Mary's, or a favorite chair in a bedroom, the charm and atmosphere of DeKoven transport visitors into a quieter and more relaxed plane of existence. Countless guests speak of the peace and solace they find here in ways unavailable elsewhere.

There is a palpable spirituality in the garths, hallways, alcoves, chapels, and walks around campus—an etherial timelessness, yes, but also a recognition, to use poet Richard Wilbur's words, that "Love calls us to the things of this world." The spirituality of DeKoven is decidedly incarnational, evoking a sense of the numinous through the materials of this life and the communal lives of those who live and visit here.

DeKoven's architecture, its magnificent art and antiques, its creaky floors and worn yet beautiful wooden railings and banisters, its sun-filled chapels, its old quadrangle with its far-away atmosphere even amidst a bustling neighborhood, its important daily work, and its evocation of things and people past—all combine to transport, and on occasion, transform human lives.

For 150 years, a place of education for the mind, recreation for the body, and spiritual reflection for the soul—DeKoven, yesterday, today, and tomorrow. Vigeat Radix: Indeed, May the Root Thrive!

Contributors List

Sister Dorcas Baker, C.S.M., has been a member of the Community of St. Mary since 1962. She and Sister Letitia, C.S.M., currently run Mary's Margin, a small house of prayer and hospitality in Mukwonago, Wisconsin. She has also led and taught International Folk, Scottish Country, and Sacred Congregational Dance for over 30 years.

Katherine Greer Clark has been volunteer program coordinator at The DeKoven Center for five years, while dividing her time with her home parish in Valparaiso, Indiana. A retired English teacher, she has been an associate of the Community of St. Mary for over 50 years. She conducts retreats and has written a number of spiritual essays for publication.

Lawrence N. Crumb is associate professor emeritus (library), University of Oregon, and currently active as an interim ministry specialist. He is the author of *The Oxford Movement and its Leaders: A Bibliography* and several articles on church history.

Mabel Benson Du Priest is professor of English at Carthage College in Kenosha, Wisconsin. Her research interests include Edmund Spenser and the English novel. She has given papers and published reviews and articles on British women novelists. She has just completed a creative nonfiction book based on her Swedish family and a novel set on Lindisfarne Island.

Travis Talmadge Du Priest is vice president of the DeKoven Foundation for Church Work and executive director of The DeKoven Center. He also serves as chaplain to the Community of St. Mary (Western Province) and confessor and spiritual director for the order of Julian of Norwich. He taught humanitites at Carthage College for 27 years, and served for 20 years as an editor of *The Living Church* magazine. He has published over 300 articles and essays, five chapbooks of poetry, and scholarly works on seventeenth-century writers Jeremy Taylor and Katherine Philips.

Jason Fout is curate of St. Paul's Episcopal Church in St. Joseph, Michigan. He is a graduate of Seabury-Western Theological Seminary. In addition to his pastoral ministry, he has an abiding interest in church history and contemporary theology.

Robert Boak Slocum is rector of the Church of the Holy Communion (Episcopal) in Lake Geneva, Wisconsin, and a lecturer in the Department of Theology at Marquette University. He is review article editor of the *Anglican Theological Review*. He is author of *The Theology of William Porcher DuBose: Life, Movement and Being;* editor of *Engaging the Spirit: Essays on the Life and Theology of the Holy Spirit;* and co-editor of *The Episcopal Dictionary of the Church.*

www.ingramcontent.com/pod-product-compliance
Lightning Source LLC
Chambersburg PA
CBHW071709180426
43192CB00051B/2096